THE USE OF MUSIC
IN
CHRISTIAN EDUCATION

THE USE OF MUSIC IN CHRISTIAN EDUCATION

Vivian Sharp Morsch

Philadelphia
THE WESTMINSTER PRESS

Library of Congress Catalog Card Number: 56-8427

PRINTED IN THE UNITED STATES OF AMERICA

CONTENTS

FOREWORD

THIS BOOK has been written with the hope that all who are concerned with the educational program of the Christian church may find that it stimulates their thinking, planning, and activity, and helps them achieve a more effective use of music. Its thesis expands the philosophy that music is like a thread that is fastened securely to the loom of educational purposes, and shuttled through the entire life of the church and program. Any consideration of the music of the church as a separate entity, or even as one that is attached to the outer periphery, is too superficial to be significant. The book sets forth a basic philosophy of music as Christian education, and applies it to the purpose of the teaching program in worship, curriculum development, program areas of faith, witness, outreach, and fellowship, and to the teaching procedures in the organizations of the church, including the church school and the choirs.

It is hoped that the book will be helpful to ministers, directors of Christian education, choir directors, members of music committees, members of Christian education committees, and church school teachers and superintendents.

The urge to write this book has grown over the years that I have been teaching in standard leadership courses, denominational leadership training schools, choir schools, laboratory schools, and presbytery workshops, along with the conviction that everyone who is responsible for any part of the music program in the church should work in the knowledge of its relationship to the total program of Christian education, and that those who are

responsible for planning total church program should be fully aware of the purpose and the significant and full uses of music. My sincere hope is that the book may help in the definition of "The Christian Educational Use of Music" as the music program for the whole church, and that it may bring choir directors, Christian educators, teachers, and ministers closer together to work out the church's program for the extension of the Kingdom.

Many people have helped in some way to make it possible to write the book. Dr. W. Lawrence Curry has been very helpful in making suggestions for topical, organizational, and repertoire inclusions. Rev. Hamlin G. Tobey has given many suggestions and constructive criticisms. My sister, Miss Mary Sharp, has given many hours of devoted assistance in the preparation of the manuscript. My mother has helped me to be selective, by listening to the endless rereadings of chapters. Mrs. Hildore Lansing, my secretary, has been of invaluable assistance in many ways, and my daughter Carol has been a constant inspiration and boost to my morale, through her loving concern and faith in me.

My husband has shared his ideas and experiences with me so completely that they are our common property and so this book is lovingly dedicated to Chester.

VIVIAN MORSCH

Chapter 1

MUSIC — A LANGUAGE OF RELIGION

MAN, in all his relationships, is subject to his powers of communication. The level of his culture, his intelligence, and his spiritual power reflect the adequacy of his ability to communicate to God and to his fellow man his thoughts, emotions, spiritual yearnings, and fulfillments. Over and over again it has been proved that music can speak, with meaning and power, of a spiritual experience too deep for verbal expression.

Truly beautiful music is a vitally important medium of religious expression. It can speak of an indefinable, intangible, purely spiritual quality of religious experience which is beyond the words with which we voice our thoughts and beyond the emotions stirred by rhythm and pretty tunes. It can open a door into "another world," a world of pure spirit. In the words of Frederick William Schlieder (*Beyond the Tonal Horizon of Music,* p. 5):

> "Music is a state approaching
> God-ness. It is a word of cosmic
> Dimensions without boundary save
> The imaginary expanse of eternity.
> There is no place where it is not.
> Its plan is hidden in the atom, and
> Concealed in the heavens.
> In man's soul is felt the design of
> Celestial splendor.
> Goethe exclaims, 'Yes, I see it ever

> Clearer; the eternal and fundamental
> Chord of our inner life is God-ness
> Itself.' "

Pleasurable experiences with beautiful music make us more keenly sensitive to all beauty. When we enjoy music, our emotions are heightened, our hearts are warmed, and our whole being becomes more sensitive. We are more aware of the beauty in the song of a bird, a flash of color, the texture of a petal, or the warm clasp of a hand. And strangely enough, this kind of experience with music rarely ever takes hold of a person when he sits alone, listening to music. A symphony shared with a loved one, or with enthusiastic listeners, in a crowded hall, is more beautiful because it is a shared experience. A large group of choir children gathered together in festival spirit to worship through song can become so inspired that their voices will take on a quality hitherto not noticeable. Through music the children are able to communicate their devotion and love and to pour forth in song their spiritual yearnings and joys. Such an experience can linger with one for days, making the participant more warmly receptive to all beauty, more purely loving in all relationships. Out of antiquity comes the wonderful story of the dedication of Solomon's Temple: "And it was the duty of the trumpeters and singers to make themselves heard in unison in praise and thanksgiving to the Lord, and when the song was raised, with trumpets and cymbals and other musical instruments, in praise to the Lord, 'For he is good, for his steadfast love endures for ever,' the house, the house of the Lord, was filled with a cloud, so that the priests could not stand to minister because of the cloud; for the glory of the Lord filled the house of God." (II Chron. 5:13, 14.) God himself spoke through the music, communicating with his people.

We ask ourselves what it is that makes people respond in this way to some music. Does the power lie completely within the music itself? If so, then why are some people transported into a world of spiritual ecstasy when listening to the Bach *B Minor Mass* while others are bored? Why do some people have only a

shallow emotional response to music, preferring a pretty tune or a catchy rhythm?

"There is something so potent and elemental in the appeal which music makes that it is possible to derive pleasure from even an unwilling hearing or a hearing unaccompanied by effort at analysis; but real appreciation of its beauty, which means recognition of the qualities which put it in the realm of art, is conditioned upon intelligent hearing. The higher the intelligence, the keener will be the enjoyment, if the former be directed to the spiritual side as well as the material." (H. E. Krehbiel, *How to Listen to Music,* p. 15.)

Daniel Gregory Mason makes this statement concerning differences in the ability to appreciate music: "Each individual in developing his taste passes naturally from song to symphony. Each can climb only by his own activity, there is no riding on the shoulders of others. Each has limits set upon him by his own nature beyond which he cannot go, and it is no discredit to him to stop where his honest opinion holds him." (*From Song to Symphony,* by Daniel Gregory Mason. Used by permission. Copyright, 1924, by Oliver Ditson Co.)

The fact that music has continued, down through history, to speak to man of God and to be the language through which man has tried to express his religious thoughts and feelings is evidence enough that music is a very important religious expression. The examination of the historic relationship of music to religion can tell us many things. In the Middle Ages, when the Roman clergy were more absorbed with quibbling over theological differences than they were with men's souls, the music became cold, mechanically involved, and as foreign to the people as the Latin of the service which they could not understand. The music of the Lutheran Reformation was a language of the people, speaking with strength and conviction of the faith for which they fought. The music of Johann Sebastian Bach, dedicated "to the glory of God," continues to speak grandly, sincerely, and convincingly of the beauty of the pure in spirit. Some music heard in churches today speaks neither of eternal truth nor of lasting beauty.

That church music has appealed to the senses or has emotionally stirred the listener or participant is not in itself evidence of a religious experience. The spiritual and emotional responses to music are so intertwined with the aesthetic that it is impossible to determine the point at which an aesthetic experience transfers over into one that is religious. But this transfer can be so effective as to make music the one most important agent for the inducing of religious experiences.

The relationship of music to worship is not its only historical and powerful one in the church, for music has also been used to teach and strengthen the faith. That the early Christians used music for the purposes of Christian education is evident in Paul's letter to the Colossians (ch. 3:16) in which he directs them to teach and admonish one another in psalms and hymns and spiritual songs, singing with grace in their hearts. It is a known fact that knowledge gained through a pleasant experience and in the framework of rhythm and melody is more deeply impressed and more lasting in the memory than mere words. Commercial advertising has followed this principle in the use of theme songs on radio and television. It has also been acknowledged that more doctrine and theology are taught through hymns and songs than through sermons or Sunday church school lessons.

Because of the historically important relationship that it bears to religion and because of the power it has always had to induce and condition the quality of religious experience, music deserves a more serious and basic consideration by our churches than it sometimes gets. Like the frosting on a cake or ornamentation superimposed on a building for little more reason than that it is handsome, music is frequently added to the program of the church.

The large number of choir systems in our country trained by skilled musical directors and beautifying the worship services of our churches is evidence that our Protestant Christians recognize the importance of music in worship and in the church program. It would be difficult to overestimate the contribution of these organizations to the lives of the participants and to the program

of the church. Artistic training and expressional outlet are obtainable to people who care to avail themselves of their musical opportunities. Our services are more beautiful and spiritually rich because of the excellent quality of our choirs. Moreover, choirs have helped, to some extent, to improve congregational participation in hymn singing.

Many churches have sought to lift the aesthetic level of congregational appreciation and participation by concentrating their efforts and music budgets upon choirs. Elaborate choir systems are helping to train large numbers of American singers to express religion through their voices, and yet countless people will never experience the power of a beautiful song because their ability to respond has not been awakened and guided through high-level participation experiences. Even in churches that are fortunate enough to have choirs for all who will accept the privilege of membership, only a relatively small percentage of the congregation is directly involved in the organizations that provide participation experiences for growth in musical appreciation.

We live in a world full of a myriad of sounds and sights which the average man does not hear or see. Radios and televisions blare out their advertisements, counters are strewn with comics, tabloids, and pictorial magazines, all bearing testimony to the faith men have in the power of rhythm and melody, color and graphic composition to stimulate men to activity. By paying a small sum of money one can purchase a lurid comic book or a book of poetry. By the simple act of turning a dial, one can select either a symphony orchestra or a bebop band. It is all a matter of choice. There is so much sensory stimulation surrounding us day and night that we have ceased to see or to hear anything. We are no longer aware of the fine distinctions between sounds.

In churches there is more good music available than ever before. There are well-trained musicians, good instruments, and larger music budgets, and yet ears are so accustomed to what they hear over the air continually that congregations fail to discriminate between the relative appropriateness to a worship serv-

ice of a Bach choral prelude, an operatic air, or a sentimental love tune. Church choirs spend months preparing to sing great music like Brahms's *German Requiem* or a Bach cantata and there are church members who will not leave their television sets to share in the production. Bach walked a hundred miles to hear Buxtehude play the organ. Organs of our day are grander, more magnificent, and tonally more varied and beautiful than those of Bach's day. There are opportunities available to hear artist organists within easy driving distance in most sections of our country. Obviously, availability of good music does not, in itself, increase appreciation.

We need only to step into the average Sunday church school department and listen to the listless, toneless singing to realize that little if any plan (or thought) has gone into the use and integration of the music into the church school program and that the leaders have no understanding of the potency of music as an instrument of Christian education. Not infrequently is the quality of the musical selection poor and unrelated as well. Even the choir members in the group, sensing the difference between the levels of musical experience, give lip service only and contribute little to vitalize or make meaningful the music of the school.

A large number of the city churches of the country employ skilled, highly trained musicians to administer their choir programs and to work with the ministers in enriching the worship services with the beauty of music. It is not uncommon for this fine music to fall upon unappreciative ears and unaffected hearts because the congregation is incapable of a sympathetic response. If the music of the choirs is to lift men's souls through the beauty of its expression, then churches must plan to educate the congregation as well as the singer. If we recognize the fact that music can condition and qualify the religious experiences with which it is associated, then we should also admit that it is of the utmost importance for the church to find and supply ways of extending participation experiences in good religious music to reach into every group of every age level in the church.

To the oft-quoted educational principle, " We learn by doing "

could be added the equally true statement, "Participation increases appreciation." Both statements are especially true concerning music. Our sensitivity and the completeness with which we can give ourselves in response to music are increased by a pleasurable experience in making music. Taking even a very small part in a group production of beautiful music can actually raise the level of appreciation. If the group production is artistic, the individual participant has the spiritual experience of an artist. Robert Shaw, well-known contemporary choral director, has said: "I believe that the choral art is the natural spiritual and artistic expression of a democratic people . . . a firsthand creative experience, open to all men of vision, honest effort, and good will. To be an artist is not the intellectual luxury of a few, but the spiritual necessity of us all." (Quotation used by permission.)

An active listening experience is one in which the listener participates with his mind, emotions, and spirit, even though he is not physically producing the music. When we listen to music that we have at some time actually produced, our listening participation is greatly increased. Unless we develop a higher percentage of listener participation in congregations, it is doubtful if even a magnificent rendition of music can lead the congregations into high-level worship experiences. The highest level of church music can never be attained, nor can its purposes be fulfilled, until congregations can recognize it and understand it as a means of communication with God and man.

Chapter 2

MUSIC AND WORSHIP

THE MUSIC of the church is an integral part of its common worship and can be apprehended, and appreciated in its true perspective, only when this is understood. To consider the music of the church worship service except in the light of its historic relationship to worship, and as stemming from God, would be superficial and profane.

Music is related to worship because the art of music is the most truly divine of the arts, the most mystical and the purest expression of worship that man has discovered.

" The God who made the world and everything in it, being Lord of heaven and earth, does not live in shrines made by man, nor is he served by human hands, as though he needed anything, since he himself gives to all men life and breath and everything. And he made from one every nation of men to live on all the face of the earth, having determined allotted periods and the boundaries of their habitation, that they should seek God, in the hope that they might feel after him and find him. Yet he is not far from each one of us, for

" ' In him we live and move and have our being ';

as even some of your poets have said,

' For we are indeed his offspring.' " (Acts 17:24–28.)

Man is drawn by God into worship and adoration of the Creator in whose image he has been made, for God is the initiator of the worship relationship and man is called upon to glorify

him with his entire being. Man's life is made up of opportunities to choose between glorifying his creator or separating himself from the life-giving God. Our Bible is full of evidences that the God who created all things in heaven and earth made man, his creature, to "feel after him and find him," and, having done this, to "live and move and have . . . [his] being" in him. "Finding" has always driven man to worship, and to long to apprehend the Spirit, God.

It is not man's needs and wishes that first evoke worship. It is God alone who matters, and God's Presence which incites man's soul to respond in adoration. When adoration starts to stir in man's heart and he begins to be aware of the absolute purity of God, he recognizes the sinfulness and impurity of his own soul, and he cries out in penitence and petition to God to cleanse him and make him worthy. In humility he offers up his sacrifice to God, emptying himself of his sins. The cleansing power of joyful adoration replaces that of guilt.

Man is not a solitary creature, for God has placed him not only in families but in communities as well. In worship, man's whole nature responds to God, his social as well as his personal. Together, men contrive sensible and visible expressions for their corporate worship. In a united effort to give beauty of artistic form to their common worship, men devise liturgies. Every sensible means at man's disposal is played upon to make more lovely his offerings of praise. The rhythm of music, poetry, and bodily movement; the warmth of rich color in fabric and glass; the beauty of structure of both temple and cathedral—all are manifestations of man's deep need for corporate worship.

From the first crude altar before which Abraham offered his praise and sacrifice to the ornate Temple built by Solomon, in which thousands of the Children of Israel made a joyful noise on loud trumpets and other instruments of music, and sang, "For he is good, for his steadfast love endures for ever," is a long progression in the development of man's use of the arts in the worship of God. But in all the history of worship there has never been recorded a more perfectly expressed description of worship

than that recorded in the Old Testament: "Holy, holy, holy is the Lord of hosts; the whole earth is full of his glory," cried one seraphim to another, "and the glory of the Lord filled the temple" (Isa. 6:2, 3; II Chron. 7:1). This Sanctus, the most perfect hymn of adoration, has often been referred to as the "essence of worship." The worship experience described by Isaiah has been generally accepted as the process through which man worships God, and is basically the underlying pattern of all services of worship from that of the Hebrew Temple to those of the present-day Protestant churches. The pattern framework progresses from man's adoration of God in his holiness, through man's humiliation for his sinful unworthiness, God's forgiving power, to the offering of his life in dedication to God's glorification through service.

Christian worship has its focal point in devotion to the person, life, teachings, and sacramental presence of Jesus Christ, through whom God has chosen to reveal himself in history. Christian worship is always directed toward the purification of life. The Christian prays with the psalmist, "Create in me a clean heart, O God; and renew a right spirit within me" (Ps. 51:10), and strives for a spiritual oneness with God, which he may never attain, but which is set before him as a beacon light by the Christ whom he follows. Christian devotion is an act of faith, for truly sincere worship implies belief in the God who is the Father, the Son who is the Revelation, and the Holy Spirit who is the Guide.

James D. Smart states in his book *The Teaching Ministry of the Church* (pp. 119, 120) that "education into the Church is initiation into a worshiping community. Before the Church can do anything or say anything, it must have its being, and it has its being in worship, which is its humble, grateful response to God who, by his Word, has called it into being. . . . Worship is the Christian's vital breath."

If worship is the "vital breath" of the Christian life, music is the heart of the service in which Christians worship, for music gives the pulse by which the life and vitality of the people's worship response is maintained. Music is the most social of the arts,

as well as the most mystical, and hence the most nearly perfect medium for corporate worship. It blends the emotions of the people into one formal, unified outpouring to God, furnishing personal outlet without embarrassment or self-consciousness. Music makes a participant of the worshiper, and helps him to apprehend the meaning of the worship experience as it stimulates his religious feeling and makes spiritual perception keener. For music works two ways in the participant: while it impresses and stimulates him, it also incites him to expression. The effectiveness of the music as an expression of devotion is dependent on the acceptance of it by the worshiper as his own sincere expression.

The Christian Church has a rich heritage of music in worship which came from the Hebrew Temple. It is obvious that the first Christians used the Hebrew psalms for their own religious devotions. These psalms have remained, down through history, the most important body of poetic, religious expression. It became apparent very early that songs were needed in praise of Jesus Christ, and as early as the second century, Christian hymns made their appearance.

Both the greater and lesser doxologies (Gloria in Excelsis Deo and Gloria Patri) were in use during the second century. The former is the first Christmas hymn of the Church and was ordained by Telesphorus in A.D. 129 to be sung in all public church services. "In the Holy Night of the Nativity of our Lord and Saviour, all shall celebrate public church services, and in them shall all solemnly sing the 'Angel's Hymn.'" The earliest form of the Gloria Patri was "Glory be to the Father, through the Son and in the Holy Spirit," which, when contrasted with the Sanctus, makes one aware of a difference between the Hebrew and the Christian conception of worship. To the Christian, God is not less holy than he is to the Orthodox Jew, but more perfectly revealed in his holiness through Jesus Christ, and he seems less remote because the Holy Spirit is with us to guide us.

From the time the Christians, driven from the Temple and synagogues, began to worship entirely apart from their orthodox brothers and began to make converts of the Gentiles a distinctly

Christian liturgy began to be formed, using the familiar Hebrew heritage with its emphasis on the ancient poetry of psalms and canticles, and Scripture, and superimposing on that structure the distinctly Christian ceremony of the Eucharist. Their service was divided into two parts, the first of which was centered around the reading and expounding of Scripture, the recital of prayers, and the singing of psalms, hymns, and canticles. To this first service the catechumens were admitted, and they learned Christian worship while participating in the company of believers. The second and more truly Christian part of the service took place after the catechumens had left and the doors were barred. The celebration of the Eucharist was a commemoration of the sacrificial death of Jesus, and came to be celebrated with a conviction of the mystical presence of the living Lord. From the beginning, the Holy Mystery of the Eucharistic ceremony was the central act of Christian worship and was obligatory to all believers. It was always an act of the group but at the same time the means of personal communion. As the Church came to realize all its implications, the Eucharistic celebration grew in richness and beauty. Through the long history of Christendom these two strands of worship have persisted in the life of the Church, the prophetic and the sacramental; the uttered Word and the living Presence. The Catholic and predominantly liturgical churches have adhered strongly to sacramental emphasis, and the Evangelical Protestants have restored the prophetic strand while retaining the Eucharistic commemoration. The celebration of the Eucharist remains in some form in all truly Christian churches and is the only permanent and deeply significant element which Christianity added to the Jewish liturgy.

The Psalter was the hymnal beloved and used by Jesus himself in his worship of the Father, and for this reason, were there none other, it should be considered the most important body of Christian musical literature in existence. Early in the Christian Era, the words of the lesser doxology, " Glory be to the Father, and to the Son, and to the Holy Ghost; as it was in the beginning, is now, and ever shall be, world without end. Amen," were added to the

psalms, as a stanza, and gave the Christian stamp of approval to the psalms used in worship services. Not only did the words make the psalms Christian, but they served as a constant reminder that Christian worship is finally directed to God, the source of being in the eternal triune Deity.

The music of the Christian Church should always point the worshiper in this way to God. Nothing of it should be out of harmony with this great purpose of worship.

From these beginnings has risen the magnificent institution, the Universal Christian Church. Like a great tree, it has branched out more and more as it has grown older and stronger. It remains alive and sturdy because it derives its life from Jesus Christ, the taproot. Some of the branches, more than others, lay stress on formal worship, some on freedom, some on sacrament, some on symbol, some on prophecy, some on evangelism, but with few exceptions they regard music as an important integral part of common worship. The form and the emphasis differ, but the focal point of worship does not alter. Jesus Christ still points the way to the Father who made us, so that we might "feel after him and find him. . . . 'For we are indeed his offspring.'" Music is an important way to glorify God, the Father, the Son, and the Holy Spirit.

It is important that this conception of worship, which is our Christian heritage, be transmitted to the children and youths of our churches, for educating for worship is the most important of all the purposes of Christian education. Worship is best learned in the family, the church, the church school, and the choir.

Parents who seek after God and find him and who live and move and have their being in him can teach their families the true meaning of glorifying God. From the family worship experience they will feel drawn to the social expression of worship in the larger family of the church. Here the children will learn with the help of their parents as they participate in common worship.

Dr. James Smart aptly points out in *The Teaching Ministry of the Church* that all adult worshipers are teaching worship by

example, whether or not they realize it. A child who attends church and observes unenthusiastic, nonparticipating members is not likely to gain the idea that worship is for the glorification of God. If the nonparticipating adults happen to be his parents and add bigoted criticisms to the first injury, the child is likely to become highly indifferent to common worship or even openly antagonistic.

The church worship service itself can teach much about worship. A child responds to orderly arrangement and to beauty more than to preaching or direct teaching. A worship service that is little more than a collection of detached miscellaneous parts preceding the minister's sermon can do little to bestir a sense of worship in a child or an adult. Music selected to glorify an organist's technique or a singer's voice, or just because a choir likes it, will only encourage the worshiper to stay away, when he does not like the singer or the music.

An excellent place to learn the purposes of worship is in a choir. The choir is dedicated to this purpose and, when led by a devoted director, participates heartily in a worship service, with understanding and reverence. Such a choir director teaches the singers the church's form of worship and helps them to use it.

The church school curriculum should, and probably does, include a unit of study on the meaning and forms of worship. When the unit occurs, the teacher has a glorious teaching opportunity. He may consult with the minister and choir director about the history of worship and the part music has played in that history and invite one or both of them to visit the department to enrich the study with music or other materials and to share from their specialized training and experience.

Worship services in the school furnish learning situations. As soon as children are old enough to take part in planning for and participating in them, they will learn greatly from the experience. The teacher will guide them to be thoughtful and thorough in preparation, selecting and practicing the music and Scripture readings best suited to the theme or the part of the service in which they are to be used. Church school worship services must

be planned and presented with serious purpose if children are to learn the true meaning of worship.

If the music of the worship service is to evoke the intended response from the worshiper, he should know why the music is used and what is expected of him in return.

The music of the service has an important function in helping to carry the whole service forward. All of the music should advance the thought of the service, and at the same time prepare the way for the next part. It can tie the whole period of worship together in a better unity than can be achieved in any other way. At every point in the service where it is used, the music must create the mood most sympathetic to that part.

A great deal of the smoothness of the progression of the service depends on the organist and his sensitive selection and use of interludes, modulations, and other instrumental offerings. When he has done his work well, the worshiper is not consciously aware of it. He feels uplifted only by the service in which he was able to worship with his whole being. It is when the organist is not at his best and the music is inappropriate, jarring on the worshiper (consciously or unconsciously), that he is most likely to notice it.

Instrumental bridges aid the smooth continuity of the service. Interludes and modulations from one key to another require a great deal of study and practice in order to make them effective. Few organists can improvise music that does not call attention to itself or its composer. The interludes are more important to the flow of the service than the prelude and the postlude. They are bridges and should be selected to carry the worshiper emotionally from the preceding part of the service into the next part without shock to the sensitivities. Contrary to popular belief, interludes do not exist in the service to facilitate the seating of late-comers or to give the minister a "breather."

The bridge that precedes the anthem is a short musical period that carries the listener from the previous act of worship into the mood of the anthem. This is necessary only when the change may otherwise be too abrupt. It occurs most frequently at the

time of the offering. The longer instrumental offerings have purpose also. The term " prelude " is really a misnomer, for this musical selection is offered as a preparation for worship and as such should be given adequate regard by the congregation, the minister, and the organist. To quote Waldo Selden Pratt (*The Problems of Music in the Church,* p. 13), " Its object is to suffuse a general atmosphere of reverence, and through the power of tone to knit together those present into unity of feeling." If the tones of the organ merely serve to cover the confusion of late entrance and friendly conversation, abruptly terminating with the entrance of the minister and choir, the effect and purpose are lost. The congregation should be taught the purpose of the prelude and encouraged by every method to give it its right use.

The postlude suffers greater misuse than the prelude. With the final " Amen " of the benediction, American worshipers arise and depart, but not until they have lingered long enough to shout friendly greetings above the organ. The organist, not to be outdone, puts on full organ and in a determined fury plays the music he has been practicing all week to " waste its sweetness upon the desert air." In some churches the congregations have the custom of remaining seated for a short meditation after the benediction, during which the organist plays softly. The organist allows enough time for a short prayer and then brings the " postlude " to a fitting close. The worshiper leaves with the dignity befitting his recent experience.

The choir, in addition to its function of leading the congregation in its musical participation, sings short portions of the service which give accent to the meaning and mood. In nonliturgical churches the amount and kind of choral portions differ according to the needs of the service and the ability of the choir. They may include an introit (a hymn or short motet to set the mood for the beginning of the service in adoration), a choral call to worship, a call to prayer, a response to prayer, the versicles (responses to sentences by the minister), a response to Scriptures, an offertory response, an orison (a prayer hymn), a choral benediction, and choral amens. These choral portions may add great

beauty to a service when they are thoroughly prepared and are sung with religious feeling. The interpretation should be worked out to fit the meaning and use in the service. Appropriate tempo, volume, phrasing, and diction contribute to their beauty of rendition. Some hymnals have a section of responses in them.

Anthems are choral compositions that are used to heighten the emotion of the worshiper. The congregation should participate vicariously in the rendition, and experience the emotional and spiritual response appropriate to the part of the service in which the anthem occurs. If anthems are always sung in the same place in the service, the repertoire will be limited to anthems appropriate to that act of worship. One church always uses an anthem early in the service and hence is limited to the use of short praise anthems. Many churches use the anthem close to the sermon to heighten its emotional effect.

The choral repertoire should be selected with the same care for theology, poetry, and musical taste that should be exerted in the selection of hymns.

Chapter 3

THE STUDY OF HYMNS

THE CHRISTIAN HYMNALS that we use come to us through a glorious growth from roots as deep as man's worship of the one true God; they are hallowed by psalms used by Jesus Christ himself, and greatly enriched by the poetic records of experiences of Christian men and women who have been guided by the Holy Spirit. Men have suffered and died that we might have the privilege of singing Christian hymns today in our Protestant churches. How can we regard lightly the significance of the position of the hymnal in the life and worship of the church, or how can we confine our use of the hymnal to the one small section of hymns which are the product of the past century, ignoring the glorious hymns that unite the saints of all ages?

Some years ago, Dr. Oliver Beltz, of Northwestern University, made this statement: "At the bottom of most of these difficulties are two main factors—the failure to give the hymnal its larger place in the life of the people and the absence of a program of education in church hymnody and its appreciation. The pastor's preparation for carrying on this work in a quiet, effective way will bring a reward as definite as it is certain, not only in terms of better singing, but in increasing ability of the congregation to appropriate fully the message of its hymns." (*The Minister and the Hymnal,* p. 16.)

Hymns must be studied and learned, to be loved and appreciated. They must be known if they are to be used as vehicles for worship. Hymns form the major portion of the literature of

religious music, and, as such, should be considered the backbone of the music repertoire of the entire church. They should be sung, enjoyed, studied, and talked about at home and in the organizations of the church, especially in the church school and choirs.

There are several approaches to the study of hymns which will lead to a better understanding and use of the hymn literature.

I. *The Topical Approach*

Most hymnals have been arranged according to topical classification. A glance at the topical index of the book will suggest several approaches to hymn study. One of the most obvious is a study of hymns in relation to the parts of the worship service in use in the church. This is called the topical approach.

Using the general pattern of worship that is in common use in Protestant churches—(1) Adoration—Praise; (2) Penitence—Confession; (3) Assurance of Pardon; (4) Illumination; (5) Self-offering—Consecration—one may learn much about hymns by evaluating their fitness to the place in the service in which they are to be used. "Joyful, Joyful, We Adore Thee," by Henry van Dyke, set to Beethoven's stirring tune, rings out with contagious, joyful spirit in praise of the Father and the Son, a perfect expression of adoration. Used in the wrong place in a service, the emotional effect would be damaged; for example, as a hymn of confession. Bernard of Clairvaux wrote a hymn in the twelfth century, the beauty of which has withstood translations through two languages to become our hymn. "O Sacred Head, Now Wounded, with Grief and Shame Weighed Down," used in the right context, makes the singer feel, with Bernard of Clairvaux, humility and shame for his transgressions. Used early in the service, without emotional preparation, it would lessen the sincerity and depth of the feeling response. Thoughtful attempts to select suitable hymns to relate to the parts of the service in which they are to be used will greatly increase the appreciation.

II. *The Historical Approach*

The historical approach to hymn study fits well into the church school curriculum materials for children and adults. The history of hymns is inherent in the history of the Church and of worship.

The major movements within the Christian Church have each produced a characteristic hymn literature, which has in time been assimilated into a common treasury of hymns, used by men of most denominations today. Some of these movements, along with hymns from them which are in use, are listed here:

1. The psalms in their various settings and adaptations provide the Hebrew background base for all hymnology.

2. The first songs of the Christian Era are found in the New Testament in The Gospel According to Luke — the three canticles of the incarnation: the Magnificat, the Benedictus, and the Nunc Dimittis. Very early in the Christian Church the two Glorias (Gloria in Excelsis Deo and Gloria Patri et Filio) were added to the Sanctus, of Biblical derivation, and have continued in use to our day.

3. One of the oldest Christian liturgies, the liturgy of Saint James, was written in A.D. 347. It was supposedly devised for the church in Jerusalem, written in Greek, and became the basis for the Eastern Orthodox liturgy. From this liturgy comes an exquisite gem of a Eucharistic hymn. It is lovely in its English translation, set to the French tune "Picardy," and is beloved by children and adults.

> "Let all mortal flesh keep silence,
> And with fear and trembling stand;
> Ponder nothing earthly-minded,
> For with blessing in His hand,
> Christ our God to earth descendeth,
> Our full homage to demand."

4. From the early Greek Church we inherit two beautiful hymns from its Evening Service of Lights: "Hail, Gladdening

Light, of His Pure Glory Poured" and "O Gladsome Light, O Grace of God the Father's Face."

5. From the early Latin Church comes a beautiful hymn of the fourth century by a Spaniard, Aurelius Clemens Prudentius. "Of the Father's Love Begotten, Ere the Worlds Began to Be" is a glorious combination of pure adoration and theological teaching, consistent with the Christian's conception of worship.

"O Come, O Come, Emmanuel" is a translation of a twelfth century Latin hymn set to a thirteenth century plain song tune.

"Jesus Christ Is Risen Today" is based on a Latin hymn of the fourteenth century.

6. The German Lutheran Reformation contributed to our hymnody many chorales of strength and beauty, but none is more beloved than Martin Luther's tender Christmas chorale.

> "Ah, dearest Jesus, holy Child,
> Make Thee a bed, soft, undefiled
> Within my heart, that it may be
> A quiet chamber kept for Thee."

7. The Genevan Church was more severe in its adherence to the prophetic strand of worship. Hymns had their place and the psalms were the accepted hymns. The best known of the Genevan psalms is William Kethe's metrical version of Psalm One Hundred, "All People That on Earth Do Dwell," to Louis Bourgeois's tune, "Old Hundredth."

8. The Scottish Church followed the Calvin tradition in its use of psalms and developed its own Psalter. Dear to the hearts of Scottish Presbyterians is the metrical setting of the Twenty-third Psalm, "The Lord's My Shepherd, I'll Not Want."

9. The Church of England followed more closely the tradition of the Roman Catholic Church and developed its liturgy with chants and hymns. England has produced some of the greatest hymns we sing. Isaac Watts's "Our God, Our Help in Ages Past, Our Hope for Years to Come" is one of the grandest hymns of the Christian Church.

10. The early Methodists were prolific hymn writers. "Jesus, Lover of My Soul" is one of Charles Wesley's 6,500 hymns, and a prized gift from the Methodists to our historic treasury.

11. Each new age brings fresh impetus to Christians to create their own songs of praise. In 1845, from the pen of an American poet, James Russell Lowell, came the stirring lines, "Once to Every Man and Nation Comes the Moment to Decide." The twentieth century gave us William Pierson Merrill's challenging "Rise Up, O Men of God! Have Done with Lesser Things."

Other religious movements have made their contributions of hymns. Among the most noteworthy contributions not listed here are those of the Moravians.

The stories of hymns and the periods of history in which they were produced are so related that they should not be separated in studying them. The hymn "A Mighty Fortress Is Our God" by Martin Luther is best understood and appreciated in the light of its history. This great paraphrase of Psalm Forty-six became the hymn of the Reformation. It was written in 1529 for the Diet of Spires, the one in which the German princes made protest against revocation of their liberties, thus gaining the name of "Protestants." The strength of the hymn reflects the firm faith of its writer and mirrors the spirit of dauntless courage in the face of all dangerous opposition, which has characterized true Christians of all ages of history, but was especially present in the first Protestants.

III. *The Theological Approach*

The minister and the Christian educator, at least, must be concerned with the theology of the hymnal. The evidence is strong that the theological concepts set forth in hymns make deep and lasting impressions on people. This is one of the good reasons for denominational hymnals and one of the very special reasons for the use of graded hymnals in the teaching program. Since they have been carefully edited with theology in mind, teachers would do well to adhere closely to the hymns designated by their denominations to be sure that the doctrine is suitable for the age

of the pupils. Theological entanglements caused by hymns render the hymns useless for teaching and even harmful.

The sureness of God's loving concern for his children, his continual presence, and his wisdom in answering prayer are well described in the anonymous hymn-poem "The Lord Is Ever Near" (in *Hymns for Junior Worship,* No. 75). Here is a concept of a God who is not remote, but always with us and always sure in his loving concern.

"The Lord is ever near, He bids His children pray;
While they are speaking He will hear, And bless them day by day.

"Our Father's love is sure, And very wise His care;
He gives us what He knows is best, And hears our every prayer."

IV. *The Poetic Approach*

The hymnal is a book of beautiful poetic literature and warrants careful study as such. Many of the great poets have contributed poems of rare beauty, which will greatly enrich our lives if we but read and learn from them. For personal and group devotional use they are unequaled by any literature save the Bible. Dr. Beltz tells us that "anyone with but an average appreciation for poetic imagery, and with only a meager understanding of the things of the spirit, will find food for thought in our hymns." (*The Minister and the Hymnal,* p. 14.)

Although it is difficult to give rules by which good poetry can be evaluated, there are a few general suggestions to help in selection:

1. Does the poem express beauty through its imagery, choice of words, and rhythmic flow?
2. Does it reflect the originality and inspiration of the poet?
3. Does it inspire its audience to an experience that does not end with the poem? Is it worthy of a place in the memory because it can continue to inspire with frequent recollections? Is it powerful?
4. Does it communicate eternal truth and beauty from poet to

audience or does it merely express the poet? Is it universal in its appeal?

5. Is the message clear?

Christina Rossetti's poetry is of the stuff that makes music in the soul before the musician has turned it into song. "Love Came Down at Christmas" is such a poem. In the beauty of simplicity she speaks of the loveliness and the theology of God's gift of his Son far more adequately than many theological treatises on the subject, for these words will be remembered.

"Love came down at Christmas,
 Love all lovely, Love divine;
Love was born at Christmas,
 Stars and angels gave the sign.

"Worship we the Godhead,
 Love incarnate, Love divine;
Worship we our Jesus:
 But wherewith for sacred sign?

"Love shall be our token,
 Love be yours and love be mine,
Love to God and all men,
 Love for plea and gift and sign."

V. *The Musical Approach*

The music of hymns is a study in itself, and no appraisal of the hymnbook can be complete without recognizing the importance and worth of the music. Only one who has attempted to harmonize a melody, in hymn style, can fully appreciate this type of music. To write according to strict rules for four-part harmony, to keep it from sounding labored, and to make all the parts interesting, constitutes quite an order. The music and the words must match in mood and message. This law is frequently violated when hymn poetry is mated to music of the same meter, regardless of quality of feeling. Also, music and words must match in placement of accents. Consider the hymn to the tune "O Quanta Qualia":

"Bless-ing and hon-or and glo-ry and power,
Wis-dom and rich-es and strength ever-more
Give ye to Him who our bat-tle hath won,
Whose are the King-dom, the crown, and the throne."
Horatius Bonar.

Note that the rhythm of words and music flow forward in one strong movement. Now sing the hymn "Be Still, My Soul" to the tune "Finlandia" (Sibelius) and then scan the poetry, placing the accents on the words where they fall in the music. You will note an awkwardness.

"Be still my soul, the Lord is on thy si-ide
Bear patient-ly, the cross of grief or pain."
Katharina von Schlegel;
Trans. by Jane Laurie Borthwick.

There is a historic heritage of the music as well as of the poetry of the hymns. Few hymns in our Evangelical hymnals are dated earlier than the thirteenth century. The tune of "Tonus Perigrinus" is supposed by some authorities to be the tune of the psalm sung by Jesus on the night of the Last Supper. If it is, it may well be the oldest "Christian" hymn tune we have.

The Methodist hymnal contains a setting of the Lord's Prayer to a Gregorian chant, which is one of the very successful uses of a Gregorian tune, used authentically because of the prose style of the words. Probably one of the reasons that our Protestant churches do not use more plain chant tunes is that the music of the Roman Catholic Church was of a nature peculiarly suited to the requirements of the Mass. In some instances, it has been successfully adapted and arranged to suit English poetry. The twelfth century plain song in Mode V, "Divinum Mysterium," lends itself well to the narrative poetry of "Of the Father's Love Begotten" and is one of the best examples of an adapted plain tune. "Veni Emmanuel" comes from the thirteenth century, and "Deo Gracias," the Agincourt Song, is dated 1415.

Most of the truly great composers since the Protestant Reforma-

tion (some from before) are represented in the contemporary hymnals. There are Palestrina, Mozart, Haydn, Bach, Handel, Beethoven, Brahms, Mendelssohn, Schumann, Purcell, Tallis, Holst, and R. Vaughan Williams, with a host of others. There are folk tunes so old that their origins have been lost.

The hymnal is a collection of good music which may be used by itself for the purpose of inducing religious atmosphere and preparation for worship. This music is used effectively for listening enjoyment and to produce religious moods and attitudes.

Many different methods have been employed to make hymn singing a vital experience of the faith of people as individuals and as congregations. A continuous planned program for the study of hymns in the Sunday church school and choirs is one of the most effective means. The morning worship services will reflect the growth that is made in this program area. Hymns should be thoroughly learned and stored in the memory in the junior department church school and choir. Units of study according to the suggested "approaches" may be made in youth groups, weekday classes, and adult organizations.

The following additional devices have proved helpful in promoting enthusiasm for hymn singing:

1. Church leaflets may carry annotations about hymns and their writers.
2. Ministers may tell briefly about the hymns to be sung in services.
3. Repetition of a hymn on several successive Sundays helps to familiarize the congregation with it.
4. A new hymn may first be presented by the choir, as an anthem, or by a soloist.
5. The congregation may practice singing at informal meetings.
6. Hymns should be related to other teaching materials in many ways. Many psalms and other Scripture passages have been set to music. "O Worship the King" is a hymn paraphrase of Psalm One Hundred and Four. A parallel study of the psalm and the hymn should prove interesting. Hymns may be illustrated on posters or friezes as an activity to stimulate

interest and promote better understanding of the meaning of the words. Primary, junior, and junior high children will all enjoy this method.

7. The music of hymns may be used without the words, with nursery and kindergarten children, to suggest moods and feelings, and to relate to picture materials.
8. Creating a hymn, either words or music, or both, is a splendid way to gain appreciation of hymns, and to feel the joy of creative activity.
9. Hymn festivals can be a large-scale means of popularizing hymns and they have been growing in popularity. They are held by one church, a denominational group of churches, or as a community project. Children's, youth, or adult hymn festivals can all be thrilling events. In the local church there is no festival more interesting than a family hymn festival, which whole families attend and participate in together. Preparation is made and the hymns are practiced in the individual age level organizations and in the homes.

It is difficult to find hymns which the entire family (all ages) knows and can sing together. The following list of twenty-five hymns is submitted, with the suggestion that everyone, from the primary department on up, can participate in at least the tune and probably one stanza of each. They represent the historic periods and movements of the Christian Church, as well as many of the great hymn writers.

A List of Twenty-five Hymns to Grow On

1. "All People That on Earth Do Dwell" — "Old Hundredth"
   William Kethe — Louis Bourgeois, Genevan Psalter
2. The Doxology — "Old Hundredth"
   Thomas Ken
3. "Men and Children Everywhere" — "Rock of Ages"
   John J. Moment — Ancient Hebrew Melody, arr. by Charlotte Lockwood Garden
4. "When Morning Gilds the Skies" — "Laudes Domini"
   German — trans. by Edward Caswall — Joseph Barnby

5. "Joyful, Joyful, We Adore Thee" Henry van Dyke	"Hymn to Joy" Ludwig van Beethoven
6. "All Creatures of Our God and King" Francis of Assisi	"Lasst uns erfreuen" *Geistliche Kirchengesäng*
7. "This Is My Father's World" Maltbie D. Babcock	"Terra Beata" Franklin L. Sheppard
8. "For the Beauty of the Earth" Folliott S. Pierpoint	"Dix" Conrad Kocher
9. "O Come, All Ye Faithful" Latin — trans. by Frederick Oakeley	"Adeste Fidelis" J. F. Wade's "Cantus Diversi"
10. "Silent Night! Holy Night!" Joseph Mohr	"Stille Nacht" Ascribed to Franz Grüber
11. "Away in a Manger" Anonymous	"Mueller" James R. Murray
12. "Fairest Lord Jesus" German, 17th century	"Schönster Herr Jesu" Silesian Folk Song
13. "All Glory, Laud, and Honor" Theodulph of Orleans — trans. by John Mason Neele	"St. Theodulph" Melchior Teschner
14. "Jesus Christ Is Risen Today" From the Latin, 14th century	"Easter Hymn" *Lyra Davidica*
15. "Faith of Our Fathers!" Frederick W. Faber	"St. Catherine" Henri F. Hemy
16. "Our God, Our Help in Ages Past" Psalm 90 — Isaac Watts	"St. Anne" Ascribed to William Croft
17. "Glory Be to the Father" 2d century	Scottish Chant
18. "In Christ There Is No East or West" John Oxenham	"St. Peter" Alexander R. Reinagle
19. "Now Thank We All Our God" Martin Rinkart — trans. by Catherine Winkworth	"Nun Danket" Johann Crüger
20. "We Praise Thee, O God" Julia B. C. Cory	"Kremser" Old Netherlands Melody
21. "The Lord's My Shepherd" *Scottish Psalter,* 1650	"Evan" William H. Havergal
22. "All Praise to Thee, My God, This Night" Thomas Ken	"Tallis' Canon" Thomas Tallis

23. "Hark, the Herald Angels Sing" (stanza 1 only)	"Mendelssohn"
Charles Wesley	Felix Mendelssohn
24. "How Firm a Foundation" (stanza 1 only)	"Adeste Fidelis"
"K," in Rippon's "Selection"	J. F. Wade's "Cantus Diversi"
25. "I Love Thy Kingdom, Lord"	"St. Thomas"
Timothy Dwight	"Williams' Psalmody"

Chapter 4

THE CREATIVE TEACHING OF MUSIC IN THE CHURCH SCHOOL

MUSIC has a large contribution to make to the teaching of religion in the church school. From the day when Paul wrote to the Christians at Colossae, directing them to admonish one another and to teach with psalms and songs, on down to our day, Christians have used music to serve the cause of Christian education. How effectively it has been used we cannot judge, but lives have been changed because of the powerful influence of music, and teaching has been enriched by its use.

In our day, Christian education has been undergoing considerable criticism and change in its methods of approach, and in the strength of its sure foundation of faith. The first consideration of music in the church school is its relation to the strengthening of the Christian faith and to worship. Then the way in which this is to be done becomes a matter for thorough study and improvement.

Church school education has profited well by the advances made in the field of secular education. Finger painting and rocking boats, kneading mixtures and paper tearing, are all frequent evidences of the invasion of the techniques of secular education into the church's teaching program of little children. Experiences with all kinds of materials and stimuli are considered essential for the little child. Project and workshop methods, field trips, and even role-playing are attempts to apply creativity to the teaching of older children and youths. Interest centers and committee

planning bear testimony to the Church's recognition of the fact that it is as individuals and in small groups that we are able to find the threshold of interest over which one enters into satisfying learning experiences. Children and young people are having an increasing number of happy learning experiences in churches because they are being given the opportunity to contribute to the plans for activity and are given choices among experiences which will lead to degrees of satisfaction.

In the light of this forward movement in the Church toward a democratic method of education which is consistent with the Christian ideal of democracy, it seems strange that, in the realm of music, the most potentially creative of the educational experience, there is so little application of the creative approach. With the exception of the preschool division of the church, the authoritarian, formalized total group plan of music education generally predominates.

Several factors may contribute to the reluctance of the church school leaders to experiment with or adopt the use of music methods that are consistent with the other phases of their program.

First is the small amount of time allotted for the church school session and the unwillingness of the staff to extend the time in any direction.

Second is the timidity of the leaders to try a method they have not seen demonstrated.

Third is the lack of understanding of the meaning of creative teaching in terms of constructive use of the imagination and applied to the teaching of music.

Fourth is the prevailing belief that one must have unusual musical ability or skill in order to lead others in musical experiences.

Several pages of this book have been devoted to developing the thesis that music is a most important language of religion—so important that the language should be taught to all Christians to enjoy and use. Music is so universal a language that we can safely say that it would be possible for everyone to enjoy some

kind of music experience, and that everyone has the right to find the way to enjoyment that has meaning for him.

If we look at Jesus' way of helping people to find the satisfactions that enrich life with eternal values, we will discover his rare understanding of human nature. Why are we so tardy in the application of Jesus' teachings to our own methods of dealing with people? Jesus recognized the worth of an individual and planned to build his Kingdom by influencing and winning men, one by one, drawing them as individuals into relationship with him, and at the same time into Christian fellowship with his group of disciples. He recognized the individual differences of personalities and of culture and experience backgrounds, and met people where they were, and as they were. Seeing them imaginatively for what they could become, he furnished a contact, an experience, or an idea which made all of life different for them and started them on a new adventure.

Our teaching of Christianity, by whatever means, should follow this principle of the acceptance of individual differences in people and their need for experiences which will bring them satisfaction now, and lead them on to higher forms of satisfaction. If we believe that the power to come alive to Christian experience through music lies in the hearts of all men, then how can we excuse our failure to meet the needs of individuals with experiences in music which have the power to capture their imagination and enthusiasms now, and which may develop (with creative guidance) into specialized skills which will give even greater satisfaction?

Every person is unique in his response to music experiences because of his own peculiar combination of personal qualities and experiences. So, no two people enjoy music in exactly the same way; yet music can draw people of congenial interests together in spiritual proximity as can no other shared experience. Music experiences, like religious ones, are entered into on the individual level, at the threshold of individual experience, but, upon entering, the person is drawn into the fellowship of music lovers.

Congeniality of musical appreciation is not determined by age groupings. One child of nine may have the musical ability and the accumulated musical experiences that lead to voluntary and pleasurable participation in a choir. Another child of equal musical talent may never have found his threshold of musical interest and, thoroughly disliking to sing, may be a complete nonparticipant in all of the music of the church school.

The music experiences that have been commonly offered in the church school, above the kindergarten department, have consisted mainly of singing in the church school worship service and singing in the choir. The singing in the church school departments has often been of a quality not likely to capture the imagination of a normal, lively, nine-year-old boy.

In order to enter through the doorway into a rabbit hole, Alice in Wonderland had to drink from a bottle that made her conform to the size of the hole. Too many of our church school programs are planned according to the rabbit-hole principle of fitting the child to the experience rather than the other way around. Irrespective of " size " of interest and growth, " Alice " and Johnny are forced through the same doorway into the " room " of music. If Johnny just does not care to drink from the same bottle that Alice does, he can stay on the outside of the room. In some schools, on the other hand, the attitude toward music experiences is like Goldilocks' entrance into the house of the three bears, where there were several pieces of furniture of assorted sizes from which to choose. Her investigations carried her from baby-size bowl to papa-size bowl, from baby-size chair to papa-size chair, from baby-size bed to papa-size bed, and through all the rooms of the house. Then came an abrupt end of activity, because there were no more rooms and no more furniture to explore. In the same way creative teaching stops abruptly when no more materials are provided and no more doorways stand open to beckon Goldilocks forward. What started as a thrilling adventure ends dormant in bored inactivity.

There are five kinds of music experiences through which people can enter into an active relationship with music: singing,

playing, rhythmic, listening, and creative experiences. These experiences can have meaning for people of all ages. Experiences, once limited to the very young beginner, are now regarded as equally fascinating and impelling to beginners of more mature years. This basic kind of music experience does not exist for the sake of performance, but for developing the inherent tendencies that we all have. These are the experiences through which the church school seeks to relate music to the expression of religion, from the very roots of religious education. The very most basic religious experiences can be expressed through basic musical experiences. Music and religion are related from the very first most primitive movement toward religious expression to the highest expression of pure religious feeling. To be able to pass from the initial experience of joy in a purely rhythmical expression with which man first offers his praise to God to the exalted lift of the voice with the mind and spirit in response to Beethoven's *Ode to Joy,* man has to progress through a sequence of satisfying musical experiences that prepare him for each new growth stage with stimulating participation.

The basic religious experiences, which the church school provides and which, like the music experiences, relate to all of life, are worship (the individual's response to God), prayer (communication with God), Christian fellowship (the individual's relation to each other), and learning from experience resources (the Bible, the hymnal, curriculum materials, personal example, missionary resources). Creative uses of basic experiences of music should be intertwined with the basic religious experiences so that they are completely integrated and associated with each other.

Sunday morning church school sessions of one hour duration do not offer weekly opportunity to devote much time to experiences with music that are not related, in a specific way, to other phases of the church school program. The classroom teacher, or departmental supervisor, is the person who can best guide the experiences, for he knows the teaching program and can find frequent opportunities for the use of music. The natural and spontaneous inclusion of music can be motivated by

supplying materials and resources so that they will be at hand when the opportunity arises for the experience.

An enthusiastic teacher can find ways of extending the time for music experiences by:

1. Arousing the interest of pupils to carry the experience outside of the classroom for completion, or to make preparation for the next week. This may draw the parents into the experience also.

2. Adding a presession or postsession on an informal experimental basis, the children participating at will. Materials can be laid out and the teacher should be on hand to help (only as needed) the pupil to try out new ideas, evaluate and relate and apply them. To illustrate both 1 and 2:

The National Mission theme for the year 1955–1956 was "Indian Americans." The junior department had copies of the reading book *Yakima Boy,* by Grace W. McGavran (Friendship Press, 1952), as well as other books about Indians on the reading table in the book nook. Old copies of *Missionary Mail* and of *The National Geographic Magazine* containing pictures of American Indians stood temptingly near some scissors, paste, and a scrapbook on another table. In a third nook of the room were some pictures of Indian instruments and Satis N. Coleman's book *Creative Music for Children.* A few materials were on this table — a small earthen bowl, a few small boxes with covers, a few beans, some sand (or salt), some pebbles. Teachers, one to a table, were near the tables. As the children came into the room before Sunday church school, they were drawn, as if with magnets, to the interesting tables. The music table discussion centered around the kind of musical instruments the Indians used and what their music is like. A junior choir boy knew something about the music because the choir had been learning " 'Twas in the Moon of Wintertime " (found in *The Gift Is Rich,* by E. Russell Carter (Friendship Press, 1955). It was decided that some percussion instruments could be made to accompany the carol and that the junior department could learn to sing it. Several children made some shakers quickly out of the boxes and filler

provided. One of the boys said he could make a drum with a nail keg that he had in the garage, if he had a drumhead. The teacher said he would supply a real skin drumhead if the boy would prepare the drum. On the next Sunday, the boy brought in a carefully painted nail keg. The teacher gave him the skin head and it was taken home to be fastened to the keg. The boy's father helped decorate the drum and decided that a second skin was needed. He provided the skin for the other end of the drum. Another child brought in a real tom-tom, others brought dried gourds. This was the start of an Indian exhibit in the department. The choir director was invited to teach the Indian carol to the department, and with tom-tom, gourd and shaker accompaniment, it was a beautiful addition to a carol program. Before the interest in the subject had waned, the missionary reading book became well-worn and the children were carrying it home by turns between Sundays in order to finish the book. In addition, many of the children were coming regularly for a half hour of extended time before the main session.

3. Adding a weekday afterschool or Saturday session.

4. Establishing a one and one-half hour or two-hour Sunday morning session.

Other times when creative experiences for all children may be, and are being made, available are in youth groups, vacation schools, camps, conferences, and weekday religious education schools.

The teacher who is timid about trying creative teaching because he has not seen it demonstrated should remember that the creative learning experience gains from the spirit of adventure, and the teacher who is learning with the pupils oftentimes gives them more of the joy of accomplishment through his own learning experience. People like to feel that the activity or the project is theirs, that they thought it up. If they not only share in the planning, but also are first over the ground, they are more enthusiastic and the satisfaction in accomplishment is greater.

The teacher who does not use creative methods because of lack of understanding should read some of the excellent material

suggested in the bibliography of this book. Satis N. Coleman, Beatrice Landeck, Beatrice Perham Krone, and James Mursell, as well as others, have made outstanding contributions to the field of creative approaches to music. The teacher should learn a few necessary principles and then learn through his experience that his function is to:

Create a stimulating environment
Encourage pupils to make their own discoveries and choices
Be ready to help pupils to relate their discoveries and apply their acquired skills to other learning situations
Keep the experiences simple (not too much teaching at one time)

The prevailing idea that unless a teacher has musical ability and skill he is not fit to lead others into musical experience can be proved erroneous only through experience. The teacher's enthusiasm and ability to give confidence and encourage others in creativity is far more important than his own skill. A resourceful teacher will have resource materials at hand and will know of someone who can supply the knowledge of skills where that is necessary. But the best person to lead the creative experience is the one who is most familiar with all the phases of the teaching program.

Creative uses of music experiences will help to achieve the goals of Christian education. The purposes of Christian education can be summarized in two simple statements: Christian education strives to win people to a growing personal relationship with God through Jesus Christ, the Holy Spirit, the Scriptures, and the Church. Christian education is concerned with better human relations in carrying out Christ's command to go teach and make disciples of all nations of men. Music experiences must be used in the church school to make religious experiences more meaningful to the individual, drawing him creatively into tune with his Creator and furnishing him a medium for the wholehearted expression of his religion. Music in the church school must also draw the individual into a Christian relationship with others, giving him a more sincere respect for and understanding

of his neighbors. The music of other people helps to bring about better understanding and sympathy. Folk song material is definitely at home in the church school. Friendship Press has given us Edith Lovell Thomas' *The Whole World Singing* and the Association for Childhood Education International, along with the National Council of Churches, has contributed *Songs Children Like*. There are many good folk song collections available.

In summary, music experiences must be furnished for everyone in the church because of their vital contributions to Christian education; creative approaches must be used to gain the wholehearted participation of everyone; creativity is the use of constructive imagination; creativity must move through the entire program relating music to every other phase; creative participation in music should be a continuous progression throughout life; music experiences in the church must stem from the same roots as religious experiences and be intertwined with them. Specialized music activities will stem from wholehearted participation; creative teaching is the democratic method of Christianity, which, recognized, respects and utilizes individual differences in ability, experience, and cultural backgrounds, and allows all an equal chance to participate; and tends to create better human relationships.

The basic experiences of music are singing, playing, rhythmic, listening, and creative. None of these experiences is isolated in its use or stands alone, for there is interplay of the basic experiences. They overlap and flow one into the other to such an extent that any consideration of purely one kind of musical experience is impossible.

Chapter 5

EXPERIENCES WITH SINGING

THE MOST commonly used approach to music is singing. Before a child is able to convey his feelings in words, he uses his voice in expressive combinations of tones and conveys his feelings to others. From infancy a child responds to the mood and feeling of song in the form of lullabies, or gay songs, in warm, loving tones. The child becomes sensitive to the rise and fall of tune and the coloring of the tone with emotion before he is aware of the words and their meanings.

The first musical experiences a child has in the church have a real and lasting effect on his attitude and feeling response to the church. A warm, gentle, loving voice can bid a child welcome, and draw him into the new relationship, through a medium to which he can respond better than he can to words.

Since a person's voice is his chief means of communication, and since practically everyone has a voice which he can use for the purpose of conveying ideas and feelings, the conclusion is that singing is the first and most important experience with music, and is within the possibility of achievement by most people, to some degree of satisfaction. Because of the peculiarly intimate and personal nature of the human voice, the satisfactions that can be derived from experiences with it exceed those of all other musical experiences. For this reason, if for no other, singing is the most important musical medium for the expression of religion; and everyone in the school should be provided with stimulating opportunities to sing and to develop his ability to

use song as his personal and social outlet and expression of emotion. Religious feelings and thoughts are sometimes difficult to express. The deeper the emotional involvement, the more need there is for its release and the harder it is to express, without embarrassment and self-consciousness. Singing can help the person to utter his thoughts and emotions with self-abandonment. His own emotion is identified with the song, and the personal nature of singing makes it possible for him to derive satisfaction from the utterance.

Singing is making tone, and the most satisfaction comes from making good tone. The church school leader will need to use considerable creative imagination to discover ways to lead the pupils into the use of the best tone possible for them to achieve, without in any way limiting the freedom and joy in participation in the song by every person in the group.

The song leader need not be a trained singer in order to help the singers to find satisfaction through song. The leader should recognize good tone and provide pleasurable opportunities for the pupils to hear it, and make it their own. It would be helpful for the teacher to practice, in private, to use his own voice according to the suggestions made in this chapter and in the chapter on voice. A few simple suggestions put into practice will usually suffice to help the teacher to lead the pupils in song and to help them, by example, to sing easily and with pleasure.

These suggestions may help the teacher to get results:

1. The child's natural singing voice is "head voice," not "chesty"—an $\overline{\text{oo}}$ tone that floats freely on the breath (like a balloon) and is focused in the head.

2. The beauty of tone is not judged by volume. It should be free from strain and "alive." Enthusiasm and vitality give tone life and color. A child's voice should never be "heavy" or raucous.

3. Erect posture, free from tension, yet alive, is essential to good tone.

4. Sincere, warm pleasure in singing and the song will color the tone with beauty.

5. Interpretation of the song through clearly enunciated words gives the song meaning.

Technical descriptions and discussions about tone production should be avoided in the church school classes, unless a discovery group leads into it of its own accord, and wishes to consult resources on the subject. In that case, the choir director or a singer should be called in as a resource leader. Such technical interest probably is an indication that the person or group is ready to move into the development of the special skill of singing and is ready for a choir, a small singing ensemble, or even for a few sessions of voice training.

It is to be remembered at all times that the purposes of singing, in the church school, will be defeated if *anything* interferes with the free, voluntary participation of the group, or with the individual's ability to use song for the un-self-conscious expression of his personal feelings and thoughts.

A soloist whose voice is neither too heavy, nor too rich with overtones, nor too unsteady with vibrato, may be invited to sing in the church school department. Her presentation of a new or a familiar song with beauty of tone and interpretation is inspirational. Phonograph recordings may be used in the same way to stimulate interest in the song, and to teach good tone indirectly. People do not know good tone unless they hear it. Listening to examples of good singing will, more than any experience, stimulate interest in singing and furnish examples.

The album *In Joyous Song,* produced in consultation with the National Council of Churches, Division of Christian Education, has some bands of songs sung by Adele Norman which illustrate very well the kind of tone production children may safely hear and imitate. Her tone is well focused, the head quality pure, the pitch accurate, and the diction clear. Nancy Carr's singing of "Hush-a-bye" is also excellent. All the bands in the album are not of equal value to use for examples of tone with children. If a singer starts a tone under pitch and slides to adjust, or has a spread tone which sounds as if the mouth were stretched wide horizontally, the voice should not be imitated. For tonal examples,

a woman's voice is to be preferred above a man's. This does not render the recordings of men's voices useless for all purposes. Actually, the recording of *In Joyous Song* is not always clear. The album remains highly useful in spite of its imperfections.

When singing becomes the means for personal and social expression and satisfies the needs for a basic expression of music and religion, then there are many ways in which it may be used creatively as Christian education:

To create attitudes, atmosphere, and moods;
To enrich curriculum materials and experiences;
To make departmental worship experiences more meaningful;
To make the worshiping fellowship of the sanctuary worship experience more personal and real because of participation through beauty of song.

Each of these ways will be discussed further, on the departmental level.

The songs that are used in the church school will need to be selected with imagination and care—imagination to select those which will stir the imaginative response and enthusiasm of the singer with full participation, and care that the song may be worth bothering to learn, and be appropriate. With young children, folk songs and games that suggest dramatizations and action, and songs that create attitudes and moods, are good. Folk songs help the older children to develop kindly attitudes of understanding and sympathy toward people of other nationalities and races. Hymns that have stood the test of time and history are apt to be good. In the chapter on objectives and standards a measuring standard has been suggested. Another source of good song material which is rarely used with church school departments is selections from anthem repertoire. Many beautiful anthems are simple enough for the entire department to sing, and too beautiful and stimulating to confine to the choirs alone. Many are settings of simple folk tunes and of hymns. The chief value from this music experience is that it provides the opportunity for everyone to participate in the production of music that is spir-

itually uplifting and aesthetically beautiful. Singers who have not the specialized skill of choir singers may, nevertheless, profit from participation in an artistic production. A beautiful performance with artistic instrumental accompaniment and experienced singers will enhance with beauty the contribution of the inexperienced singer. Whole departments and combinations of departments may join with the adult and children's choirs and with artistic instrumentalists to produce a fine music experience.

The following anthems are suggested because they may be easily taught to entire church school departments and used as anthems in the morning worship service, or in special services. The anthems are attractive and useful in correlation with general curriculum themes.

Anthems for Church School Departments

Use for Easter and in the Study of the Life of Christ:

"Once There Was a Garden Fair," by Bitgood, No. 95 in *Hymns for Primary Worship,* and *Anthems for the Junior Choir,* Book 2, p. 54 (both by The Westminster Press). The primary and junior departments sing the hymn stanzas, the junior choir and the adult choir sing the antiphonal "alleluias." A muted violin obbligato, an octave higher than the accompaniment, lends beauty.

Easter:

"In Joseph's Lovely Garden," by Dickinson (H. W. Gray Company, Inc.). Children of the junior and youth departments sing the melody in the second stanza above the humming of the adult choir.

Use with the Study of the Life of Christ and for Easter:

"Thine Is the Glory," by Handel, in *The Hymnal for Youth,* No. 106 (The Westminster Press). Use stanzas 1 and 2 only. *Anthems for the Junior Choir,* Book 3, p. 48. Junior and youth departments sing the hymn, the junior choir sings the "alleluias" and the descant, the congregation joins in the second stanza. (Note that the wording at the end of stanza 2 is not the same in both books.) Trumpets may be used effectively.

Thanksgiving and General Praise:

"Let All Things Now Living," Welsh folk tune, arranged by Katherine K. Davis (E. C. Schirmer Music Company, in the Descant Series, 1819). This unison anthem is beloved by children and adults and may be used by combinations of church school departments, junior, junior high and senior high.

Use with the Bible Study Theme and with the Creation Unit. Also a Good General Praise Anthem:

"I Sing the Mighty Power of God," by Bampton, in *Anthems for the Junior Choir,* Book 3, p. 12 (The Westminster Press). The junior and youth departments sing the hymnlike tune, the junior choir sings the descant.

Use with the Study of the Bible. Also Use for Hebrew Background in the Life of Christ and in the Study of Our Heritage from the Hebrews in the Study of the Church. It Is Also a Good General Praise Anthem:

"Psalm 150," by W. Lawrence Curry (H. W. Gray Co., Inc., 2129). Parts for trumpets and trombones are available from the publisher. The children of the primary, junior, and junior high departments sing in unison the tune "Old Hundredth" and the adult choir sings the words of Psalm One Hundred and Fifty set to very virile, easy-to-sing four-part music.

Dr. Curry's anthem may be taught to the junior department over a period of a few sessions — introduced in this manner:

"Men of all times who have worshiped the one God have praised him in music: in song and on instruments. We look to The Psalms in our Bible for glorious expressions of praise. Each book of the Psalter closes with a brief doxology, but Psalm One Hundred and Fifty closes the Psalter with a song of triumphant praise. The psalmist tells us that God is to be praised in his sanctuary and in heaven as well as earth. He is to be praised for his mighty deeds, measuring the praise in accord with the measure of his greatness. Man should praise God with appropriate music, instruments, song, and in dance. Everything that breathes should praise the Lord.

"Some thousands of years after the Hebrew psalmist sang the doxology of Psalm One Hundred and Fifty, Bishop Thomas Ken sang a doxology of praise to God (in 1692) which is distinctly a Christian doxology. Protestant churches of all denominations use his doxology in their worship services. Number 1 in *Hymns for Junior Worship* (substitute the page in the hymnal in use) uses his doxology for a third stanza. By singing the note values equal, we can make this sound as it does when we sing it in church. [*Sing the doxology in the meter used in the church services.*]

"Read the words and see how Dr. Ken answers the questions which the psalmist asked: (1) Why should we praise God? (2) Who should praise him? Does he say where God should be praised? Where do you think Bishop Ken believes God should be praised? Read the last phrase of the song. Is this a phrase that the psalmist could not add? Yes, this is distinctly a Christian doxology in praise of God the Father, the Son, and the Holy Ghost.

"Our adult choir is preparing to sing an anthem in our sanctuary which combines the doxology of Psalm One Hundred and Fifty with the doxology of Bishop Ken. Dr. Lawrence Curry, who is a well-known musician, teacher, composer, and editor of music publications, wrote this glorious praise anthem. The tape recording to which we shall listen was made in the choir rehearsal of our adult choir.

"[*Play a recording of the anthem, or, in lieu of this, have the church organist and a soloist on hand to demonstrate it.*]

"Did you hear the familiar doxology? When I play this again, sing the doxology with the choir. [*Play again and direct the singing.*]

"If we practice the anthem a few times, we may sing our doxology of praise in the sanctuary with the adult choir."

"The 150th Psalm," by César Franck (J. Fischer & Bro., 5670), may also be used. Five-year-old children may accompany the singing choir with percussion instruments.

Use with the Study Theme — The Church:

"Long Hast Thou Stood, O Church of God," by Lindeman, arranged by Katherine K. Davis. Unison chorus with descant, (E. C. Schirmer Music Company, 1765). Junior and youth departments sing stanzas 1 and 2, the adult choir joins in stanza 3. The junior choir and the sopranos of the youth choir sing the descant.

Use for Festival Occasions, Such as Children's Day or Rally Day:

"Thee, Holy Father, We Adore" ("Lasst uns erfreuen"), arranged by W. Lawrence Curry, in *The Hymnal,* Hymn 13 (use unison only), and in *Anthems for the Junior Choir,* Book 1, p. 14 (The Westminster Press). The junior and youth departments sing the hymn stanzas, the sopranos of the adult choir sing the descant, the junior choir and the youth choir sopranos sing the "alleluias."

Use with the Study of the Life of Christ. Also for General Use:

"Beautiful Saviour," by Christiansen, St. Olaf Series, 51 (Augsburg Publishing House). The primary, junior, and youth departments sing the hymn. Adult choir hums the accompaniment and sings the last page of the anthem. Because the anthem is written in a low key, D flat, it is advisable to use it a half or whole tone higher. Be careful to have the children use head tones rather than chesty ones which result from loud singing in a low range.

Chapter 6

EXPERIENCES WITH INSTRUMENTS AND CREATING MUSIC

THE PLAYING of musical instruments has been an acknowledged part of our religious heritage from the beginning of the Hebrew record in Genesis to our own time. In the fourth chapter of Genesis, the twentieth verse, it is recorded that Adah bore Jubal, the father of all who play the lyre and pipe; and in the twenty-second verse, " Zillah bore Tubal-cain; he was the forger of all instruments of bronze and iron."

A long time later in the history of the Hebrews, the psalmist sang of praising God with instruments — in Psalm One Hundred and Fifty:

" Praise the Lord!
Praise God in his sanctuary;
praise him in his mighty firmament!
Praise him for his mighty deeds;
praise him according to his exceeding greatness!

" Praise him with trumpet sound;
praise him with lute and harp!
Praise him with timbrel and dance;
praise him with strings and pipe!
Praise him with sounding cymbals;
praise him with loud clashing cymbals!
Let everything that breathes praise the Lord!
Praise the Lord! "

Reading over the instruments listed in verses three through six sounds like making an inventory of the instruments in the

music corner of a children's department of a church, and the entire psalm might well be a description of a joyful worship experience with instruments in any department of the church.

The use of musical instruments greatly widens the potentialities of happy creative participation in music. Some people enter into the love and appreciation of music through the use of instruments more readily than they do through singing, and, having discovered the joy of music through instruments, they learn to appreciate and participate in singing. The great variety and kinds of tones made possible by instruments offer appealing interest to almost everyone. The perception of tone grows keener, and the sensitivity to the fine shades of feeling expressed by different tone qualities helps to develop the musical ear and appreciation. Instruments are not a substitute for singing, but are another kind of musical experience. They expand the power of expression of thoughts and feelings and accompany song, thus greatly enriching the whole experience.

A music interest center or a music corner may be set up in a school department and be made so attractive and inviting that individual children and small interest groups will feel free to try out the tone of an instrument, to compare tonal qualities of different instruments, and to combine forces with other individuals in producing tonal effects. The instruments should be handled with proper respect and played sensitively, with attention to the tone produced, and at a time that does not interfere with other learning experiences.

A musical workshop and laboratory may be set up if a small room is available. Authentic instruments, and materials for the creation of others, may be placed on tables or shelves around the room. The laboratory may well be near the choir room or the office of a member of the staff. It should be attractively arranged according to a reasonable order. Older children, young people, and adults should have access to the room, when there is a staff person around to help, if needed, in finding resource materials and in evaluating and channeling the experiences. Besides instruments and raw materials, there should be in the

laboratory room and in the interest corner, pictures of instruments and books explaining how to produce tone. Attractively illustrated songs, mounted on durable heavy cardboard, should be left temptingly exposed for would-be instrumentalists to try. Simple folk songs and familiar church school songs and hymns should be printed on large staffs with big notes and illustrated with bright-colored pictures. Instruments should be added from time to time and others put away for a " rest."

If it is possible to buy some instruments, get good ones. It does not pay to buy any with inferior tone quality. If only a few can be purchased, buy triangles with a ringing, bell-like tone. One small cymbal that rings clearly is better than two or three with dull, thudding tones. If you buy a tambourine, select one with a good heavy skin and sturdy construction. A simple sturdy drum may be added or improvised. These instruments may be purchased from music stores that sell school instruments, or from the Educational Equipment Company, 69 West Twenty-third Street, New York 10, New York. Many instruments may be added from improvised materials. Gourds are good percussion instruments; small bells of many kinds may be procured from variety stores. Two heavy cast aluminum pan covers, which sound A and E, have done double duty in our family for many years. They ring like bells when struck with metal. Lightweight aluminum and tin lack resonant tone and do not make good cymbals. It is good to have a mixture of authentic and improvised instruments to stimulate creative ideas.

Instruments that may be added to these, for the older children, youth, and adults, are recorders, a xylophone, a chording instrument (in addition to the piano) such as a zither, a ukulele, a guitar or the recently popularized autoharp, and drums made of all kinds of materials. If the purchase of a few instruments is not feasible, the entire collection may be made or improvised.

The imaginative teacher supplies as many concrete musical experiences as possible. Experimentation with the making of instruments increases the enthusiasm and satisfaction in the playing experience. Materials of all sorts and descriptions may be

gathered together to stimulate interest in experimentation.

In the preschool and the lower primary grades, only simple instruments should be constructed. Small boxes filled with different materials provide shakers that produce a variety of tones. Use ice-cream cartons, salt boxes, matchboxes, pillboxes, and fill them with sand, salt, rice, dried peas, small stones, or other swishing sound producers. Make drums from oatmeal boxes covered with cloth and shellacked, to be played with dowel sticks tipped with cotton balls. Tambourines can be made by sewing two paper pie plates together with bright-colored yarn, and strung with bottle caps for clappers. The light metal pie plates in which frozen pies are sold make quite a joyful noise when clapped together. Rhythm sticks may be made by painting pairs of dowel sticks or small slabs of plywood. These crude instruments furnish creative satisfactions for little children and may be made at the church if there is a two-hour session, or, if not, they can be made at home and brought to church school. The instruments should be used for joyful, shared music experiences after completion. *Creative Music in the Home,* by Satis N. Coleman, contains many ideas about creating instruments. The Bibliography lists other helpful books.

Older children may experiment with making other instruments, such as a xylophone from varied-length bars of wood, a Panpipe from hollowed sticks, drums from various materials and headed with skin. Earthen bowls, metal jars, wooden boxes, woven baskets, and nail kegs make good drums and furnish adventure and satisfaction.

Change the collection of materials, adding different ones from time to time. Never use all your materials or ideas at one time. Keep back some for fresh impetus when it is needed.

People of all ages love to experiment with instruments and to construct them. When they make an instrument that really produces tone, they appreciate more fully the beautiful tone of a fine instrument. There should be a steady progression from the level of beginning experimentation to the level of ensemble experiences and accompaniment of song. The satisfactions should

increase as achievement increases. The ultimate satisfaction comes from the ability to use the specialized skill gained through experimentation and experience, to the glory of God and in his praise.

English hand-bell ringing is an ancient art, which has been introduced to American churches in recent years. The use of the bells has proved so effective in the development of increased interest in church music organization, as well as so delightful an addition to the beauty of music in worship, that the Whitechapel Bell Foundry in London, England, which casts the bells, cannot meet the demand for them. Although it is practical to have a set that ranges from $\underline{G}$ below middle C to $\overline{G}$ above octave $\overline{C}$, it is also possible to play in limited keys with a set of twelve bells ranging from C to $\overline{E}$ above octave $\overline{C}$. A sharp and F sharp are very desirable additions.

One of the most interesting features about the use of bells is that each group has to be creative in discovering the best way to secure good tone, the kind of music that is most appropriate to the instruments, how to assemble its own repertoire, and how best to make notation. There is little published about hand-bell ringing and apparently no compilation of published music. *The Book of Bells,* by Satis N. Coleman, contains an interesting history of the bells. The whole experience of hand-bell playing is a thrilling creative adventure.

Bell choirs are usually composed of enough members to allot two bells to each player. Group feeling becomes highly developed because every player is absolutely necessary to the group, if all bells are to sound. This interdependence develops a keen sensitivity to pitch and rhythm. Timing must be precise. The bell choir may produce single-line melody or harmony. Another splendid feature of the use of hand bells is that satisfaction from the playing experience results from the very first production of a single beautiful bell tone and continues to result from each stage of development of skill. Several choirs of players in one church, rehearsing at different times, may have the fun of playing the bells. There is an American Guild of English Hand-Bell Ringers

which any church group or individual may join.

Whether you praise the Lord with fine instruments requiring great skill to manipulate, or whether you make a joyful noise on a single-toned bell, do it "as unto the Lord," and your joy will be great.

Creativity is the ultimate experience in music, for through the activity one can come nearer to comprehending the divine compulsion to create than through any other experience. There is within each of us a degree of creative power which can remain dormant through life, or can be cultivated to fruition.

Divine creation is original. Human creation is a production of a work, by thought or imagination, and represents a new organization or form of existing materials. Only God is completely original.

Any new expression of a thought, a motive, or a tone color, is a kind of creation, as is any new organization of materials.

A young child who picks up a spoon and discovers for himself a satisfying rhythmic pattern has felt the first joy of creation. Children who spontaneously burst into inventive song phrases, no matter how short, how few words, or how little their word meaning, are creating a new song.

Oft-repeated words or phrases in a game or a story become intoned chant without conscious effort; and song, as soon as melody takes unconscious form.

A teacher can invent her own method of quick, unobtrusive notation of the song, and a new song has been added to the repertoire to be shared by all.

Creation of song is sometimes a conscious process, when individuals or groups invent stanzas to familiar tunes, or tunes for hymns that express their thoughts and feelings. The words need not rhyme, nor do they have to be in poetic form. Primary children can compose responses to be used in litanies or in other parts of their worship.

The simple, spontaneous experiences with invention may lead to a discussion about composition of music, with junior children.

After research into simple song form they may be guided in the refinement of their compositions. They should discover that a line of music which corresponds to a line of song is a musical phrase and they should discover the kind of cadence that does not finish the song, but, like a comma, leaves it in anticipation of the next phrase. A simple two- or four-phrase composition is a good length for the work. The junior hymnal or the church hymnal will furnish excellent examples to study. Satis N. Coleman's book *First Steps in Playing and Composing* offers suggestions for very simple composition of tunes.

Tunes may be invented for the English hand bells and other instruments. The children have keen interest in playing compositions of members of the group.

One of the most fascinating experiences in musical creation is that of fashioning musical instruments. This is discussed in the chapter on experiences with instruments.

There is a relationship between creative activities which enriches one with another. Clay modeling, finger painting, and brush painting activities are all stimulated to a greater degree with music. On the other hand, musical inventiveness is frequently released while working with creative materials.

Ways of picturing music represent another form of inventiveness. All kinds of ways have been invented over the long history of music. Our present system of notation is comparatively recent and not totally accurate or satisfactory. Experimenting with new ways is fascinating. Picture illustrations of ideas in the song, numbers, and odd symbols for notes on ladders are some ways. Children are ingenius and may invent better ones.

Since the possibilities for creative invention are limitless, children and teachers together may have delightful experiences in forming their own expressions and may "sing unto the Lord a new song." If church schools will provide opportunities for continuous, progressive experiences in creating music, not only will there be an increase in creative Christian experiences, but the field of church music may profit immeasurably by the results.

Chapter 7

RHYTHMIC EXPERIENCES

RHYTHMIC experiences have a vital contribution to make to the music of the church. Animation, strength, and joy are stimulated by rhythmic experience and full personal and social response result.

Rhythm is as fundamental to life as the pulsation of the heart or the rising of the sun. Rhythmic motion is constant throughout the universe. It is the manifestation of life created, and pulsating as part of the Creator's plan. Frederick W. Schlieder has defined rhythm in these terms: "Rhythm is the living throb in matter disclosing a purpose that God has imposed upon man and nature. The infinitesimal rhythmic impulses that bring the light of distant stars within our gaze, the majestic swing of the ocean tides, the pulsing sap of the plant, the beating of the human heart, the measure of a sentence and the span of melody — all contain a thought and desire enclosed in the vibrant pulse of an idea, and impregnated by the will to accomplish.

"Rhythm in matter is the Presence; by it things are made beautiful by holy intent. Rhythm holds the secret by which God creates: nature reveals it, man must learn it. Nature obeys it unknowingly; man, by his works, must obey it." (*Beyond the Tonal Horizon of Music.*)

Religion in its moments of deepest feeling and desires has always flowed out in rhythmic expression. When Moses led the Children of Israel out of Egypt and Pharaoh's army pursued them to the Sea of Reeds and perished, "then Miriam, the prophetess, the sister of Aaron, took a timbrel in her hand; and

all the women went out after her with timbrels and dancing" (Ex. 15:20).

The early Hebrews celebrated their victories and high festivals with song and dance. The women went out to greet the victor and played on instruments, danced, and sang. A soloist served as a precentor and the chorus joined in a refrain. It is recorded in I Sam. 18:6, 7, "As they were coming home, when David returned from slaying the Philistine, the women came out of all the cities of Israel, singing and dancing, to meet King Saul, with timbrels, with songs of joy, and with instruments of music [triangles and three-stringed instruments]. And the women sang to one another as they made merry."

On great annual festivals the Hebrews went as bands of pilgrims, marching to the Temple from all directions, to the sound of pipe and singing. Many of the psalms were used for these festival processions of the pilgrims, and were accompanied by instruments and dancing. Psalm 68:25 describes a procession in which were "the singers in front, the minstrels last, between them maidens playing timbrels." The most famous of these processionals is Psalm Twenty-four, which was sung antiphonally, with a precentor asking the questions and the people answering.

The use of the processional on festival occasions is one rhythmic expression that still prevails in many churches, while that of the more jubilant and lively dance has been largely disassociated with the Church's celebrations of festivals. Rhythm is an element of worship. The potency of devotional practice depends upon its rhythmical regularity, just as the health of the body depends upon the rhythm of the heart.

A worship service is also highly rhythmical or else it fails in its effect on the worshiper. A characteristic of worship is that there is unbroken continuity of flow, of the rise and fall of its movement. H. Plunket Greene in his *Interpretation in Song* (The Macmillan Company) says that "rhythm is like a piston; it may apparently work up and down in direction, but it drives the structure forward." (The quotation from p. 42 of the book is used with the permission of the publisher, The Macmillan Com-

pany.) This is an essential quality in a worship service, that its component parts be joined in a pulsating, flowing, rhythmic pattern, the thread of which is never broken throughout. There may be an up-and-down movement of the emphases, but the inevitable direction is always straight forward.

It is in the church school that the more physical manifestations of rhythm are most evident. The younger we are the more physical is our rhythmic expression. As we mature we are able to feel rhythm in our bodies without such evident outer expression. This does not mean that it is immature to dance, or in other ways to express rhythm with our bodies.

Rhythmic experiences should be included in a church school program for these purposes:

1. To furnish a way to learn about God. (Rhythm is a fundamental revelation of God's natural law.)
2. To furnish physical activities that enrich the emotional life and elevate the spirit.
3. To discipline the body.
4. To co-ordinate mind, body, emotions.
5. To identify the child with his physical environment.
6. To develop responsibility for learning to work in harmony with others.
7. To stimulate creativity.

Rhythmic experiences are intertwined with the other musical experiences so thoroughly that we classify them in terms of each other. They may be identified as:

1. Rhythmic experiences with song. In song dramatizations the movements are descriptive and recur rhythmically. Folk songs offer limitless possibilities for rhythmical movement. "Kuckoo," an Austrian folk song (in *Songs Children Like*), is a lively illustration. On the refrain, which imitates yodeling, there are appropriate motions, including patter on knees, clapping hands, and snapping fingers. The song is a great favorite at camps and in youth fellowship groups. "There Is No Cradle Ready," a Spanish folk song (*Hymns for Primary Worship*), is easily dramatized with rhythmic motion. Only a bit of imagination

will be needed to make a real carol in a ring, out of this Christmas folk song. The movement around the ring may be interrupted to pound with a hammer as Joseph did, and to peep at the baby, with Mary, the mother. The "Train Song," by Satis N. Coleman and Alice G. Thorn in their book *Another Singing Time* (p. 20), is an excellent example of song that lends itself to natural dramatization. In the same book, "Let's Go Walking," on p. 13, is equally useful.

2. Singing games are a kind of rhythmic song that offers change of pace in a program of the vacation school, weekday school, camp, youth fellowship, and extended Sunday church school session. The games appeal to people of all ages, because they can use their own originality in inventing stanzas and actions. They respond readily to the variety. Singing games promote the singing habit because the attention is focused upon movement and people sing freely without self-consciousness. (*American Folk Songs for Children,* by Ruth Crawford Seeger, has many songs of this type. The imagination will supply many additional stanzas to those suggested.)

Most familiar of the children's singing games are "London Bridge," "Here We Go Round the Mulberry Bush," "The Farmer in the Dell," "Did You Ever See a Lassie (Laddie)?," and the old "Here's a Ball for Baby" (in *Finger Plays,* by Emilie Poulsson). See *The Complete Nursery Song Book,* by Bertail, for familiar singing games. The more possible additions of invented stanzas, the more effective the use of the song. For older children and young people there are many singing folk games to delight the rhythmic sense and enliven a fellowship period. The American folk games "Shoo Fly" and "Jennie Crack Corn" and the German game "Ach, Ja!" are all in *Fun and Folk Songs,* revised edition, with directions for playing the games.

3. Cumulative songs are related closely to singing games. These are highly rhythmic songs which have many stanzas and in each stanza something new is added to an accumulating list. "Green Grow the Rushes-Ho" (*Fun and Folk Songs,* revised edition) is lots of fun to sing. People of all ages enjoy this kind of song.

The same pattern is followed in all these songs. In each new stanza, a part of all preceding stanzas is reiterated. A group of young people learned the twelve stanzas of "Green Grow the Rushes-Ho" at camp while drying dishes. The dishes were passed along the "production line" in rhythmic regularity and amid hearty singing.

4. Singing games create a great deal of interest when used with instruments. "The Clock Song," by Jessie L. Gaynor and arranged by W. Lawrence Curry, suggests to the imagination rhythm sticks for clock ticks. "Clap Your Hands" (*American Folk Songs for Children,* by Ruth Crawford Seeger) has a singing stanza and an instrumental one for rhythmic play. Additional stanzas may be invented.

5. Rhythmic experiences with instruments present many possibilities:

a. The instruments described in the preceding chapter should be used to accompany rhythmic movements — while some of the children play, others may interpret the rhythm with bodily movements. The children's toy instruments may be used in combination with songs or piano music in a worship service in the church school provided it is properly prepared and the proper spirit of reverence is maintained. "The Blessed Spirits," arranged by Edith Lovell Thomas from a selection from *Orpheus* by C. Gluck (in *Musical Moments in Worship,* p. 24), lends itself well to reverent use in a worship service, interpreted with toy instruments. Equally suitable is "A Chant" arranged from a nocturne by Chopin, on p. 20 of the same collection.

b. Phonograph recordings of instrumental music suggest rhythmic movements to imaginative children. This activity stimulates keen listening and helps the children to grow in their perception of the differences in rhythmic patterns, which they will translate into motion (skating, walking, and skipping). Some children may be listening while others are active. It is better for this music not to be too long. Records with small bands are well suited to this use. Some of these are suggested in the chapter on listening experiences. Two useful record collections are *Rhythm*

Activities, Victor Album E-72, and *Rhythm Activities,* Victor Album E-77.

c. The piano is the best instrument to use for this type of rhythmic activity because the pianist can adapt the music to the children and the activity. A good collection of piano music for rhythmic interpretation, and one that is not too technically difficult (a very important qualification), is *Kindergarten Book,* by Dorothy Bell Briggs, published by Oliver Ditson Co. The Briggs book has appropriate music for expressing high-stepping ponies, elephants, bears, bunnies hopping, ducks waddling, butterflies, giants, and other imitative rhythmic movements.

An older book that contains some exceptionally good instrumental music for rhythm plays, toy orchestras, dramatic and mood interpretations is the kindergarten book from The Music Hour Series, published by Silver, Burdett & Company.

Ruth Cawthorne Vesper's *Rhythmic Sketches,* Volume Two, for kindergarten and primary grades (published by The Willis Music Co., 1929), contains piano music for rhythmic interpretations and is marked for rhythm instruments.

A Pre-School Music Book, by Diller-Page (G. Schirmer, Inc.), suggests rhythmic play and rhythm band.

See the Bibliography for further suggestions.

6. The processional has already been mentioned, but it should not be passed over lightly, as a form of rhythmic expression. We have mentioned the Hebrew festival procession. Saint Chrysostom instituted the first procession in the Christian Church, to celebrate the Festival of Lights. Candlelighted processions are the most impressive of the processionals we use in our churches today. The processional adds the beauty of flowing movement and the color of pageantry to the "coming in" to a service. The appearance of the procession is fully as important as the music (if not more so). The spacing, the bodily carriage, and the rhythm of bodily movement produce beauty that satisfies the eye. If the singers move in dignified pace, bodies erect and relaxed, it should not be difficult to keep in rhythmic step. The movement of the procession is a forward one. No sideway mo-

tion can be permitted. The processional " shuffle " that is popular today is not rhythmical nor is it worthy of the name " Processional." The steps should be natural and free from stiffness. The processional should be practiced by all participants. If only the singers would remember that, besides being heard, " thy solemn processions are seen. O God, the processions of my God, my King, into the sanctuary " (Ps. 68:24), they would be more apt to move with joyful dignity befitting the occasion.

Not all rhythmic experiences, nor those most satisfying, are bodily expressions. All of the music of the church should be truly rhythmical. The very foundation of musical interpretation is a sensitivity to rhythm and a developed ability and understanding. The organist of the church has a tremendous responsibility for maintaining good rhythm. Hymns should be played and sung in good, steady rhythm. Choir experiences should be satisfying, rhythmic experiences. Psychologically, the congregation will be more likely to respond attentively to the music of the choir, so long as the thread of rhythm is not broken. When it snaps, the attention will snap with it.

Chapter 8

LISTENING EXPERIENCES

MUSIC is a tonal art which depends on aural sensitivity to transmit impressions to the mind, emotions, and body. Listening is the initial phase of every musical impression and a very necessary part of every musical expression.

A natural result of musical impression is some form of activity which involves either physical action or mental and emotional response, or both. These total responses to listening are highly desirable for children. They learn to listen more keenly when the impression is given immediate response through activity. By this process they learn how to respond to musical stimuli.

There must be some listening experiences, for people of all ages, in which the listener is quiet and allows the music to speak directly to the heart. This experience is closely akin to the religious experience of which the psalmist spoke, " Be still, and know that I am God " (Ps. 46:10). It is in outward quiet that the spirit of man apprehends God. It is when the body is inert and the mind and emotions are tuned to the sound of music that it possesses his being and he is truly aware of its meaning and significance. The experience of listening to music, in order to be possessed by its beauty, when joined to the suggestion of the psalmist makes a strong impact on the spirit. The discipline of listening to music (when so channeled) may well serve to strengthen the discipline of true worship.

Pure listening experiences may occur in the church school, the choir, the church worship services, the organizational meetings, and especially in the home.

A soloist, a pianist, an organist, a group of singers or players, or a phonograph recording may furnish the music.

The Use of Phonograph Recordings

Phonograph recordings have many uses in a church program. Wherever Christian education is going on, recordings are invaluable — in the home, the Sunday church school, youth meetings, choir rehearsals, Women's Association meetings, vacation school, weekday classes, and Family Night gatherings. A creative teacher will discover, with joy, ways to enrich teaching experiences with recordings.

By using a record player and a few choice recordings, a person's musical horizon may be extended; higher levels of artistic taste may be developed; the joy and satisfaction of artistic performance, beyond one's own ability, may be vicariously experienced; a teacher is enabled to present teaching material with a degree of artistry to which he can never attain; learning experiences may be greatly enriched and heightened.

Recordings may be used for preludes, offertories, and interludes in worship services; moods and attitudes may be created; rhythmic activities and toy bands are made effective with recordings. Songs may be taught and lessons illustrated. The imagination may be stimulated and other creative activities motivated by the use of recordings. Besides all these uses, recordings may be used just for the pleasure of listening.

In choosing recordings for use with young children, it is well to select predominantly melodic and rhythmic music. Especially suitable are those performed by solo instruments or voices, for young children " hear " solos better than ensembles. The span of attention in young children is short; hence, recordings for them should not be long. Small portions of long compositions may frequently be used effectively.

Selection of a Record Library

The church record library should be selected with great care. The best economy results when records are chosen that will have

many possible uses. The selection of recordings is based on the same standards that govern the selection of good music in education. A basic library should be chosen to include some records for all age groups and to correlate with all areas of the program and curriculum. Children respond to and absorb only the music that they can make their own. Since many people own good private collections of records, it should be easy to borrow, from time to time, records for special purposes to augment the church collection. Parts of extended works that would not ordinarily be included in a church library, because of cost, are made available in this way. For example, some movements of symphonies and concertos are suitable for worship purposes, but are not available except in albums of the complete works. The second movement of the Brahms's Violin Concerto and much of the Beethoven Ninth Symphony are uplifting and worshipful, but impossible to secure in part. A loan of the desired records will help to extend the library.

Preparation for a Lesson

In preparing for a lesson that will employ recordings, the teacher should plan carefully for their inclusion. He should:

1. Be sure the recording will speak to the need in the "spot" in which it is to be used. (Is the purpose clear?)
2. Familiarize himself with its language before presenting it to a class.
3. Adjust the record player before the class period, for volume and tone.
4. Be sure of the beginning and ending places if only a portion of the record is to be played.
5. Plan the presentation and follow-up so that the record fits smoothly into the lesson.

Teacher's Attitude

The attitude of the teacher, while listening to music, will greatly affect the class's appreciation of the music. If he is attentive and thoughtful, so will the class be. If he starts the record

player and then moves about the room, or focuses his attention on a book, looks out of the window, or in some other way distracts the attention, the class will be inattentive.

The Record Player

Record players are not necessarily expensive equipment. They may be purchased for as little as twenty-five dollars; however, it should be remembered that equipment gets hard use around an institution, and it is advisable to pay considerably more for a machine. The durability of the machine is therefore of more importance than the initial cost. It is also necessary that the record player be equipped to play records of different r.p.m. speeds. It is very desirable for each department to have its own record player. Preschool departments especially need their own, because in the very informal type of program, it is very difficult to know in advance when the machine will be most needed. It is possible, however, to so plan a schedule for the use of the equipment that one machine may be shared by the school. This does limit the use of the record library in any one department. It is wise to appoint a responsible person to care for the machine to make sure that the needle arm is fastened when it is being carried, that efficient performance is maintained, and adjustments and servicing arranged for.

Care of the Records

The records also represent a valuable investment, and adequate provision should be made for their storage. The library should be kept in one central spot, and one person should be in charge of cataloguing and loaning. A filing cabinet may be purchased or made. Records should be stored vertically and kept in a room that remains at fairly moderate temperatures at all times, to avoid warping. The record librarian should be contacted well in advance of the day on which a record is to be used in order that he may work out any conflicts in schedule that may occur.

A Long-range List Should Be Made

The task of "digging out" a sufficient list of recorded music to meet the requirements of a church's education program is harder than it should be. The National Council of Churches, Division of Christian Education, has started creating record materials and lists, but until a great many more records with small bands have been placed on the market, it will be necessary to study carefully to get the greatest value for the number of records purchased. It may take time, research, and some money to build an adequate record library, but it is one of the most rewarding of educational projects.

A "dreamer's" list could be made up as a library "at the goal" and kept posted where all may see. Gifts of money and gifts of the desired records may reward you for your effort. Build your library gradually and carefully. Maybe you can buy only one or two records a year, but be sure that they will be the two most useful ones you can buy.

A List of Phonograph Recordings for a Church

The following library of recordings has been selected on the basis of the wide use that can be made of all the records and the areas of program that the selections can serve. The list is limited and is offered as a suggestion of the way a church goes about selecting a record library for educational purposes:

Nursery Rhymes

Victor (78 R.P.M.) E-83

1. Hey Diddle Diddle; Little Bo Peep; Mary Had a Little Lamb; Little Jack Horner; See Saw Margery Daw; Ride a Cock Horse (Mother Goose-Elliot); When the Little Children Sleep (Reinecke); God Loves Me; Evening Prayer (arr. Baker-Kohlsaat)

2. Sing a Song of Sixpence; I Love Little Pussy; Pussy Cat; Hickory, Dickory, Dock; Over the Hills and Far Away; Bye-low (Traditional); Diddle, Diddle Dumpling; Wee Willie Winkie; Bean Porridge Hot

(Crowninshield); Three Blind Mice; Jack and Jill; Baa, Baa, Black Sheep (Mother Goose-Elliot)

3. John-John-Johnny (David-Johnstone); Bed in Summer from *A Child's Garden of Verses* (Stevenson-Nevin); Guardian Angels (Schumann); Golden Slumbers (Dekker-English lullaby of the seventeenth century); Cossack's Lullaby (Trans. Anon.-N. Bachmetieff); Gardens in the Sea (Manx folk tune); Indian Lullaby (Myall-Johnstone); Sleep, Baby, Sleep (German folk song—arr. from Brahms)

4. The Frog and the Mouse; The Tailor and the Mouse; The Frog He Would Awooing Go (Old English); Mr. Duck and Mr. Turkey (Riley-Gaynor); The Chicken (Riley-Gaynor); The Daisy and the Wind (Neidlinger); The Little Shoemaker (Riley-Gaynor)

Rhythm Bands

Victor (78 R.P.M.) E-90

1. Amaryllis (Ghys); Minuet in G (Paderewski)
2. Le Secret (Gautlier); Pirouette (Finck)
3. Gavotte from *Mignon* (Thomas); Rendezvous (a letter)
4. Rataplan (Donizetti); Serenata (Moszkowski); Waltz No. 5 (Koschat); With Castanets (Reinecke); Shadows (Schytte)

Rhythm Programs

Volume II, Victor (78 R.P.M.) E-72

1. Soldiers' March (Schumann); March in D Flat (Hollaender); March from *Nutcracker Suite* (Tschaikowsky); March from *Alceste* (Gluck)

2. Boating on the Lake (Kullak); Skating (Kullak); Waltzes (Gurlitt); March (Gurlitt); La Bergeronette (Burgmuller); Waltz (Schubert); Scherzo (Gurlitt); L'Arabesque (Burgmuller); Tarentelle (Saint-Saëns)

3. Run, Run, Run (Concone); Jumping (Gurlitt); Running Game (Gurlitt); Air de Ballet (Jadassohn); Waltzes Nos. 1, 2, and 9 (Brahms)

4. Praeludium (Jarnefelt); Les Pifferari (Gounod); Happy and Light of Heart, from *The Bohemian Girl* (Balfe); Tarentelle (Mendelssohn)

For Moods and Interpretation

Volume I, Victor (78 R.P.M.) E-77

1. Lullaby (Brahms); Little Sandman (Brahms); Hush, My Babe (Rousseau); Lullaby (Mozart); Cradle Song (Schubert); Sweet and Low (Barnby)

2. March of the Little Lead Soldiers (Pierné); Petite Suite (Bizet); 1-March; 2-Impromptu

3. Badinage (Herbert); Legend of the Bells (Planquette); Humoresque (Dvořák); Scherzo from Third Symphony (Beethoven); Minuet (Paderewski); Gavotte (Popper); Minuet (Beethoven); Rock-a-Bye Baby (Traditional)

4. Run, Run; Ring Around the Rosy; March, Little Soldier; Sleeping Time; Hobby Horse — "Memories of Childhood" (Pinto)

Miscellaneous

Largo from Xerxes and Meditation from Thais, Victor 12-1142 (for quiet music)

Air for the G String and Dance of the Spirits, Victor 49-3301 (for quiet music)

Ding Dong School Records — Young People's Records, Inc. Y-466; Y-467; Y-477; and Y-468

My Book, Album of Songs and Stories by Mary Edna Lloyd — Methodist Publishing House

Melodies for Children — Victor 20174

Carols for the Long Christmas, to accompany the Christmas legends from many lands in the book *The Long Christmas,* by Ruth Sawyer — Gloria Chandler Recordings, Inc.

In Clean Hay, Christmas carols and story based on "The Christmas Nightingale" by Eric P. Kelly — Gloria Chandler Recordings, Inc., 2 records

Ring Out, Christmas Bells (Organ and Chimes) — Mercury A-60 Little Town of Bethlehem; Joy to the World; It Came Upon a Midnight Clear; O Come, All Ye Faithful; Hark the Herald Angels Sing; Silent Night; White Christmas

Dutch Prayer of Thanksgiving — Victor 4322

American Bird Songs — actual recordings of bird songs, Laboratory of Ornithology, Cornell University

The Children's Corner Suite (Debussy) — Victor M-639

Music of the World's People — Audio-Master Corporation Educational Records AMC P-504: U.S.A., Greece, Eire, Japan, Madagascar, Nigeria, India, Russia, Gypsy, Bali, Iceland, Spain, Tahiti, Arabia, Tibet, France

Songs of Many Lands — Decca Album 605

Marian Anderson Sings Spirituals — Victor LM-110

Nobody Knows the Trouble I See; Ride On, King Jesus; Hear de Lam's a-Cryin'; Sinner, Please; Honor, Honor; My Lord, What a Morning; Soon-a Will Be Done; Were You There?; On Ma Journey; De Gospel Train

In Joyous Song — an album produced by the Follett Publishing Company in consultation with the Division of Christian Education of the National Council of Churches, Album RA-1

Jan Peerce Sings Hebrew Melodies — Victor 12536

Kol Nidrei; A Dudele; Eili, Eili; A Cantor for a Sabbath; A Plea to God; A Shepherd; A Dreamer; Glick; Myerke; Mein Zum

Cantorial Jewels — Columbia ML-4805

Children's Hymns and Stories — Protestant Radio Center Album 10-A

Older Primary and Junior:

Record 1 — Seeing God in Nature
This Is My Father's World (with story)
For the Beauty of the Earth

Record 2 — Palm Sunday and Easter
All Glory, Laud, and Honor (with story)
Christ the Lord Is Risen (with comment)

Record 3 — Jesus, Our Friend and Saviour
Fairest Lord Jesus
O Saviour Sweet, O Saviour Kind

Record 4 — The Good Shepherd
Saviour Like a Shepherd (with comment)
The Lord Is My Shepherd

Children's Hymns and Stories — Protestant Radio Center Album 10-C

Older Junior and Junior High, Youth, Adults (Acceptable with Older Primary):

Record 109 — The Bible:
Tell Me the Stories of Jesus

I Love to Tell the Story

Record 110 — God, Creator of the Beauty Around Us
God Who Touchest Earth with Beauty
Breathe on Me, Breath of God

Record 111 — Thanksgiving
We Gather Together to Ask the Lord's Blessing
Now Thank We All Our God

So Will We Sing — 57 hymns and anthems, National Council of the Churches of Christ in the U.S.A., Broadcasting and Film Commission, 220 Fifth Avenue, New York 1, New York

Side 1 — How Wondrous and Great Thy Works (Lyons); Rise Up, O Men of God (Festal Song); Glorious Things of Thee Are Spoken (Austrian Hymn); Praise, My Soul, the King of Heaven (Lauda Anima); Jesus Shall Reign Where'er the Sun (Duke Street); Come, Thou Almighty King (Moscow); Crown Him with Many Crown (Diademata); Rejoice, Ye Pure in Heart (Marion); Softly Now the Light of Day (Seymour); Saviour, Like a Shepherd Lead Us (Sicilian Mariners)

Side 2 — Blessed Art Thou O Lord God (W. H. Hall); How Excellent Thy Name (Handel — "Judas Maccabaeus"); Jesus Word of God Incarnate (Mozart); Rise Up, O Men of God (T. T. Noble); Gladsome Radiance (Gretchaninoff); Rejoice in the Lord Alway (Purcell); Create in Me, O God, a Pure Heart (Brahms)

Side 3 — Great Is Thy Faithfulness (Faithfulness); The Church's One Foundation (Aurelia); Holy Spirit, Truth Divine (Mercy); We've a Story to Tell to the Nations (Message); O Master, Let Me Walk with Thee (Maryton); Spirit of the Living God; My Master Was So Very Poor (Herongate); Lord, Dismiss Us with Thy Blessing (Sicilian Mariners)

Side 4 — Saviour, Again to Thy Dear Name We Raise (Ellers); Now Thank We All Our God (Nun Danket); A Mighty Fortress Is Our God (Ein' feste Burg); Thy Word, O Lord, Like Gentle Dews (St. Leonard); When Morning Gilds the Skies (Laudes Domini); All Hail the Power of Jesus' Name (Coronation); My Faith Looks Up to Thee (Olivet); Beautiful Saviour (Schönster Herr Jesu)

Side 5 — My Faith Looks Up to Thee (Olivet); Stand Up, Stand Up for Jesus (Webb); Hark! Hark, My Soul (Pilgrims); Ten Thousand Times Ten Thousand (Alford); Rock of Ages, Cleft for Me (Toplady); O Jesus, Thou Art Standing (St. Hilda); O God, Our Help in Ages Past (St. Anne); Love Divine, All Loves Excelling (Love Divine); Fairest Lord Jesus (Schönster Herr Jesu); He Leadeth Me (Aughton)

Side 6 — O Come Let Us Worship (Rhea); Come Ye and Worship (Saminsky); Doxology (Old Hundredth); Glory Be to the Father (Gloria Patri); Hear Our Prayer, O Lord (Whelpton); Almighty Father, Hear Our Prayer (Mendelssohn); Sevenfold Amen (Lutkin); Dresden Amen; Send Out Thy Light (Gounod); The Lord Bless You and Keep You (Lutkin); Now the Day Is Over (Merrial); God Be with You Till We Meet Again; Blest Be the Tie That Binds (Boylston); Break Thou the Bread of Life (Bread of Life)

Sacred Music Around the Church Year — Trapp Family Singers, Concert Hall Society, Gold Label Series CHS 1100, New York (33⅓ r.p.m.)

Sanctus and Benedictus; Maria Durck Eim Dornwald Ging; Psallite Unigenito; Jesu Redemptor Omnium; Resonet in Laudibus; O Bone Jesu; Jesu, Salvator Mundi; O Salutaris Hostia; Wer leucht' uns denn bei der finsterin Nacht?; Crux Fidelis; Tenebrae Factae Sunt; Surrexit Pastor Bonus; Regina Coeli, Laetare; To Thee the Holy Ghost; O Maria Diana Stella; Salve Regina

A Treasury of Easter Songs (Shaw Chorale) — Victor LM-1201

Christmas Hymns and Carols (Shaw Chorale) — Victor LM-1112

Christmas with the Trapp Family Singers — Yuletide songs of many lands, Vol. 2, Decca Long Play DL-9689

Organ Music (Bach-Daquin-Biggs) — Victor M-616

Stokowski Conducts Bach — Victor LM-1176 (33⅓ r.p.m.)

Suite No. 2 in B Minor; Chorale from "Easter Cantata"; Little Fugue in G Minor; Wir glauben all' an einen Gott; Come, Sweet Death; Jesu, Joy of Man's Desiring; Sheep May Safely Graze

Eleven Choral Preludes for Organ (Brahms), Opus 122 (33⅓ r.p.m.), played by Ernest White, long-playing Mercury Classics MG-10070

Mein Jesu, der du mich; Herzliebster Jesu; O Welt, ich muss dich lassen; Herzlich tut mich erfreuen; Schmücke dich, O liebe

Seele; O wie selig, seid ihr doch, ihr frommen; O Gott, du frommer Gott; Es ist ein Ros' entsprungen; Herzlich tut mich verlangen I; Herzlich tut mich verlangen II; O Welt, ich muss dich lassen II

Music of Jubilee (Bach) — E. Power Biggs, organ and chamber orchestra, Columbia ML-4435 (33⅓ r.p.m.)

Sinfonia to Cantata No. 29; Chorale Prelude: In Dulci Jubilo; Chorale Prelude: Rejoice, Beloved Christians; Concerto and Chorale: "Alleluia" from the Christmas Cantata No. 142; Chorale: Jesu, Joy of Man's Desiring, Cantata 147; Chorale Prelude: In Dulci Jubilo Fantasia; Chorale: Now Christ Doth End in Triumph, from the Christmas Oratorio; Sheep May Safely Graze, from the Birthday Cantata; Chorale Prelude: Now Thank We All Our God, from Cantata 79; Sonata to Cantata 182; Chorale: Awake, Thou Wintry Earth, from Cantata 129

The King of the Instruments — Vol. 1, Aeolian Skinner Company, Boston 25, Mass.

The Messiah — Columbia LP — SL-151 (ML-4110)

Elijah — Columbia LP — SL-155 (ML-4184)

German Requiem (Brahms) — Victor LM-6004

St. Matthew Passion (Bach) — Victor Bluebird Classics, a Hi-Fi recording, LBC-6101

Addresses of Record Companies

Aeolian Skinner Company, Boston 25, Mass.

Audio-Master Corporation, Educational Records, 341 Madison Avenue, New York 17, N.Y.

Broadcasting and Film Commission, 220 Fifth Avenue, New York 1, N.Y.

Columbia Recording Corporation, 799 Seventh Avenue, New York 19, N.Y.

Concert Hall Society, 250 W. 57th Street, New York 19, N.Y.

Cornell University, 124 Roberts Place, Cornell Heights, Ithaca, N.Y.

Decca Records, 50 W. 57th Street, New York 19, N.Y.

Follett Publishing Company, 1257 S. Washington Avenue, Chicago, Ill.

Gloria Chandler Recordings, Inc., 422½ W. 46th Street, New York 19, N.Y.

Mercury Records, 228 N. LaSalle Street, Chicago 1, Ill.

Methodist Publishing House, 810 Broadway, Nashville 2, Tenn.
Protestant Radio Center, 712 Henry Grady Building, Atlanta 3, Ga.
RCA Victor, Division of Radio Corporation of America, Camden, N.J.
Young People's Records, Inc., 27 Thompson Street, New York 13, N.Y.

Chapter 9

THE GRADED USE OF RECORDINGS

THE FOLLOWING are some of the uses, in the different age level groups, for the records listed in Chapter 8. They are not offered with the intention of setting limitations but so that they may serve to stimulate the reader's own imagination in creative teaching.

Records for Nursery

1. My Book, Album of Songs and Stories by Mary Edna Lloyd — Methodist Publishing House, Nashville 2, Tennessee
2. Nursery Rhymes — Victor Album E-83
3. Lullabies: Cradle Song; Sweet and Low; Little Sandman; Hush, My Babe — Victor 22160
4. Lullabies — in Victor Album E-77, Record 1
5. American Bird Songs — Laboratory of Ornithology, Cornell University
6. Ring Out, Christmas Bells — Mercury A-60
7. Rhythm Activities — Victor Album E-72
8. Ding Dong School — Young People's Records, Inc. Y-466; Y-467; Y-477; and Y-468

Records for Kindergarten

Use numbers 2, 3, 4, 5, and 7, in addition to:

9. The Children's Corner Suite (Debussy) — Victor M-639
10. In Joyous Song — Follett Publishing Company, Album RA-1, Record 1: I Love Little Pussy; Little Friends; Twinkle, Twinkle, Little Star; Hush-a-bye; Sky Music; The Child Jesus; God Loves Me; Sun and Stars; All Things Bright and Beautiful

11. Dutch Prayer of Thanksgiving — Victor 4322 (quiet music)
12. Rhythm Bands — Victor E-90
13. Rhythms — Vol. I, Victor E-77 (complete)
14. Air for the G String; Dance of the Spirits — Victor 49-3301
15. Largo from Xerxes; Meditation from Thais — Victor 12-1142

Uses of Records in the Nursery and Kindergarten

Listening to the story that the music tells.

Dramatizing the story; imitating animals or characters suggested by the music.

Expressing rhythmically: running, skipping, skating, dancing, hopping, flying, floating, etc.

Playing toy percussion instruments with records. This develops discrimination of differences in types of music and the suitability of the instrumentation. Develops rhythmic sense.

Inducing moods for rest, activities, worship.

Stimulating creativity. Drawing, painting, clay modeling are activities that are frequently inspired by music.

A group of four-year-old children in the church weekday nursery were working with finger paint; the RCA Victor Record Album E-71, band 2 on record 5003-B (Adagio by Correlli), was played, without calling verbal attention to it. The children began to move their arms in large, relaxed, free movements. Ann, blind since birth, asked for paper and paint. Ecstatic pleasure was reflected in her face as she was able to combine two sensory experiences. Finger painting was no longer only a tactual experience, it had become an expression of an aural and rhythmical experience.

Record 5000-B (Scherzo from "Midsummer Night's Dream") was then played. Arms began to move quickly in perfect rhythm. George reflected the instrumentation in his movements; quick movements were replaced by pointer finger line-making, when solo instruments were played. Jean responded to the rhythm with her whole body and painted with vigorous delight. The sense of touch, so keen in the very young, had been given a new

direction and impetus through the musical association; satisfac tion in the experience was increased.

Listening quietly for enjoyment and for learning.

Worshiping — short instrumental selections.

Playing — singing games.

Records for Primary

16. In Joyous Song — Album RA-1
    Record 2: Glad That I Live Am I; O Master of the Loving Heart; At Work Beside His Father's Bench; For the Beauty of the Earth; Winter Song; Bird's Return
    Record 3: Lord, I Want to Be a Christian
    Record 4: Fairest Lord Jesus
17. Sheep May Safely Graze, in "Music of Jubilee" (Bach) — Columbia ML-4435
18. Jesu, Joy of Man's Desiring — same record
19. Now Thank We All Our God — same record
20. Es ist ein Ros' entsprungen — on Brahms's Eleven Choral Preludes — Mercury MG-10070
21. He Shall Feed His Flock } The Messiah —
22. Pastoral Symphony } Columbia — ML-4110
23. If with All Your Hearts } Elijah — Columbia — ML-4184
24. O Rest in the Lord }
25. Air for the G String and Dance of the Spirits, Victor 49-3301
26. Largo from Xerxes and Meditation from Thais, Victor 12-1142
27. Jan Peerce Sings Hebrew Melodies — Victor 12536
28. Carols from "The Long Christmas" — Gloria Chandler Recordings, Inc.

Numbers 3, 4, 5, 6, 7, 9, 11, 12, and 13 of the nursery and kindergarten series, in certain situations, are useful with primary children; for example, in vacation school, weekday classes, and extended sessions.

Uses of Records in the Primary Department

For learning new hymns. The teacher and children may listen together to an artistic first presentation. Greater interest in learning the hymn results. Number 16 is suggested.

For illustrating a lesson. For example, the Hebrew melodies may be used in connection with lessons about Nazareth and Jesus' childhood.

For worshiping. Preludes, interludes, and other quiet meditation periods; numbers 17, 18, 19, 20, 22, 25 and 26 are suggested.

For quiet listening, for pure enjoyment.

For dramatizing.

For using as background in choral recitation of a psalm. For example, an excerpt from the "Pastoral Symphony" of *The Messiah* played softly for the Twenty-third Psalm. An alternative selection would be "Sheep May Safely Graze." "Now Thank We All Our God" from the record "Music for Jubilee" is in the mood of Psalm One Hundred.

"He Shall Feed His Flock." In many lands shepherds come down from their hillsides to play and sing carols each year at Christmas time. They play on bagpipes and crude reed horns. In Italy they come a month before Christmas to sing their simple carols to the citizens of the towns. They are given many gifts of food and money which they carry home on Christmas Day. From the city of Naples, Italy, comes one of the oldest and most beautiful of these bagpipe songs, "On That Most Blessed Night" (in *Noels, a Collection of Christmas Carols,* by Marx and Anne Oberndoerffer; H. T. FitzSimons Co., Chicago, 1932). George Frederick Handel heard the song about two hundred years ago and liked it so well that he used it for a contralto solo in his music called *The Messiah,* which is about Jesus. (The solo is in the album ML-4110 Columbia LP.)

(The carol and "He Shall Feed His Flock" could both be recorded on a tape and played in the class period. Have on the picture easel the picture of the Good Shepherd. This presentation should involve discussion of what a good shepherd does.)

For stimulating activity.

For pleasurable listening and learning, seasonal music.

Records for Juniors

29. Eleven Choral Preludes for Organ (Brahms), Opus 122—Mercury MG-10070
30. Music of Jubilee (Bach)—Columbia ML-4435—Organ and orchestra
31. Marian Anderson Sings Spirituals—Victor LM-110
32. Music of the World's People—Audio-Master Corporation Educational Records AMC P-504
33. Songs of Many Lands—Decca Album 605
34. In Joyous Song—Follett Publishing Company RA-1
    Record 3: We, Thy People, Praise Thee; Christ the Lord Is Risen Today; This Is My Father's World; Lord, I Want to Be a Christian; Now Thank We All Our God
    Record 4: All Creatures of Our God and King; Joyful, Joyful, We Adore Thee; Fairest Lord Jesus; All Glory, Laud, and Honor
35. So Will We Sing—National Council of the Churches of Christ in the U.S.A., Broadcasting and Film Commission, 220 Fifth Avenue, New York 1, New York. The hymns on these recordings should be carefully selected to meet the requirements set up in the chapter on the selection of music. All good hymns are not equally useful at this age level.
36. Cantorial Jewels (10 Hebrew prayers)—Columbia ML-4805
37. Jan Peerce Sings Hebrew Melodies—Victor 12536
38. Organ Music (Bach-Daquin-Biggs)—Victor M-616
39. Christmas Hymns and Carols (Shaw Chorale)—Victor LM-1112
40. A Treasury of Easter Songs (Shaw Chorale)—Victor LM-1201
41. Stokowski Conducts Bach (Vol. II)—Victor LM-1176
    Jesu, Joy of Man's Desiring; Sheep May Safely Graze; Chorale from "Easter Cantata"
42. Sacred Music Around the Church Year (Trapp Family Singers)—Concert Hall Society CHS-1100
43. The Messiah (Handel)—Columbia LP—SL-151 (ML-4110) (The sequence of recitatives telling the story from Luke: "There Were Shepherds," and through the chorus "And the

Glory"; "He Shall Feed His Flock"; "Come Unto Him"; "Hallelujah Chorus")

44. Elijah — Columbia LP — SL-155 (ML-4184)
(The "Rain" sequence, starting with No. 10 and ending "Thanks Be to God"; also "Ye People, Rend Your Hearts" and "If with All Your Hearts")

Uses of Records with Juniors

To teach about other nationalities and races (correlating with the missionary program) to develop world friendship. Numbers 31, 32, 33, and 39 are suggested.

To study the life of Jesus.

To study the history of the Church through hymns.

To learn new hymns. (Use selections from numbers 34 and 35.)

To provide instrumental music for worship services.

To listen in order to learn.

To create a background for choral speech.

To provide an atmospheric background in the same mood, use band 6 of Victor LM-1176 (Stokowski Conducts Bach, Vol. II), "Sheep May Safely Graze," with the recitation of the Twenty-third Psalm. Start the music playing, and use for an introduction the first portion, which ends in a cadence and slight ritard. With the entrance of the violin melody, start the recitation. Gently, gradually taper down the volume to the entrance of the voices. If the psalm recitation is unhurried, the music and the recitation will end about the same time.

To help learn Scripture.

To teach Bible stories.

To learn about the Bible.

Records for Youths and Adults

45. Cantorial Jewels — Columbia ML-4805
46. Organ Music (Bach-Daquin-Biggs) — Victor M-616
47. So Will We Sing — 57 hymns and anthems, National Council of Churches Album

48. Christmas Hymns and Carols (Shaw Chorale) — Victor LM-1112
49. A Treasury of Easter Songs (Shaw Chorale) — Victor LM-1201
50. Stokowski Conducts Bach (Vol. II) — Victor LM-1176
51. Sacred Music Around the Church Year (Trapp Family) — CHS-1100
52. Eleven Choral Preludes for Organ (Brahms), Opus 122 — MG-10070
53. Christmas with the Trapp Family — Decca DL-9689
54. Music of Jubilee (Bach) — Columbia ML-4435
55. St. Matthew Passion (Bach) — Victor LBC-6101
56. German Requiem (Brahms) — Victor LM-6004
57. The King of the Instruments — Aeolian Skinner Company — for the study of the organ; useful in preparing people for a demonstration of the organ; also with a series of programs on the history of the organ
58. The Messiah — Columbia LP — ML-4110
59. Elijah — Columbia LP — ML-4184
60. Songs of Many Lands — Decca 605
61. Music of the World's People — Audio-Master Corporation AMC P-504
62. Marian Anderson Sings Spirituals — Victor LM-110

Uses of Records with Youths and Adults

To study music of other peoples, to stimulate world friendship, and to correlate with missionary studies.

To study the message of the great oratorios.

To show the history of the Church.

To show the music of the Bible.

To portray the life of Christ in music.

To provide inspiration for worship.

To provide seasonal music — useful in classes, in fellowship groups, and at other church meetings.

To aid the choir. For inspiration and learning of music which the choir is to sing. For example:

In preparing the youth choirs to be the ripieno choir in the first chorus of Bach's *St. Matthew Passion,* the recording was helpful in two ways. It helped them to auralize what else was to be going on while they were singing and to give them an inspirational introduction to the grandeur of the music. One rehearsal of the two choirs, youth and adult, together with the orchestra, sufficed after the learning experience with the record.

Illustration of the Use of Recordings in a Program

The following is a program on Easter music to be presented to a group of adults or high school students, using recordings.

Play "Awake, Thou Wintry Earth" (Bach), Columbia LP ML-4435, side 2, band 5. After playing this introductory music, a reader introduces a series of selections of Easter music as follows:

Easter is the oldest of the Christian festivals, for its observance dates back to the Apostolic Age. It has always been known as the most joyous of all festivals. Many of the Easter customs derive from the heathen Eostre, so named because the spring sun had its new birth in the east. When Christianity reached the Teutonic people they naturally related their ancient festival of the resurrection of the sun to the resurrection of the Sun of Righteousness. Customs and traditions of the pagan festival were easily transferred to the Christian festival.

Easter eggs, games, fires, and laughter all have pagan origin, but early Christians eager to cast off the austerity of Lenten practices, adopted them for the joyous celebration of Easter. People exchanged the Easter kiss and greeted each other with "Christ is risen!" to which the reply was "He is risen indeed!"

Music has always had a large part in the celebration of the joyous festival of Easter. Some of the oldest carols are Easter carols. One of the oldest of the carol hymns, still sung to the original melody, is "O Filii et Filiae," sung to an altered plain song melody of the fifteenth century and translated by John Mason Neale.

Play LM 1201 Victor, "A Treasury of Easter Songs," side 2, band 8.

From the fourteenth century comes the Easter hymn best known and beloved of all, "Jesus Christ Is Risen Today." The verses first appeared in three German and Bohemian manuscripts of the fourteenth century. The tune has been ascribed to various composers. Tune and words first appeared together in 1708 in *Lyra Davidica.*

Play LM 1201, side 1, band 1.

Since Easter carols are folk music and reflect the customs and traditions of a national group, we find in them many strange local observances. For example, the Easter egg is a symbol most universally associated with the festival. In many lands, during the Easter festival, hard-boiled eggs, dyed bright colors, are the customary food. In old Russia the people used to carry eggs to exchange with friends. From Russia comes the "Carol of the Easter Eggs."

Play LM 1201, side 2, band 3.

From seventeenth century Germany comes "Hilariter."

Play LM 1201, side 1, band 2.

From Scotland comes "On Easter Morn at Break of Day."

Play LM 1202, side 2, band 6.

The American Negro has contributed two Easter spirituals in characteristic "spiritual" style:

"Do-don't Touch-a My Garment."

Play LM 1201, side 1, band 6.

"Calvary."

Play LM 1201, side 2, band 9.

The Moravians of Bethlehem, Pennsylvania, have a most beautiful observance of the Easter festival. At 7:30 on Easter Eve, the congregation start the Easter Eve watch. Many of them do not sleep on the night before Easter. Prayer, talk, and song continue until three in the morning, when a trombone choir starts on a

tour of the town, playing carols and calling the people to the morning watch in the cemetery. The people gather to sing, with the brass choir and singing choir, just as the sun rises. The Moravians are well known for their interpretations of Bach chorales.

Play "Ah, Lord, Thy Dear Sweet Angels Bend" from The Passion According to St. John *by Bach. Play LM-1201, side 2, band 10.*

End by playing "My Spirit, Be Joyful" from the Easter Cantata No. 146 (*Bach*)*, Columbia record ML-4435, side 2, band 1.*

Chapter 10

MUSIC EXPERIENCES IN THE AGE GROUPS OF THE CHURCH SCHOOL

PRESCHOOL

Singing Experiences:

Small children are sensitive to the message and warmth of feeling in a teacher's singing voice. First attitudes toward the church are affected by the emotion reflected in the teacher's voice. The child gains satisfaction through his vocal response.

Songs are included at any time in the program and are related to any part or activity. They motivate, heighten, and enrich experiences, create attitudes and moods.

A few short, one-idea songs make up the repertoire of three-year-olds. As they grow into the kindergarten the repertoire increases in number and length of song.

Children learn by repetition of songs used in meaningful situations. They join in.

Many three-year-olds do not sing a tune. The pleasure is more important. Gradually experience helps them to improve. By five years they probably will have found their singing voices and the "head tone."

The voice range is limited to less than an octave from F (above middle C) to E above. The melody should not lie too close to either extreme.

Playing Experiences:

A music center is set up with a few percussion instruments, for free experimentation at times when it will not interfere with other people and other activities.

Nursery children experiment as individuals and sometimes come together in very small groups to play together, chiefly spontaneously.

Kindergarten children find playing together in groups more natural and satisfying.

Songs are accompanied, at times, with light, simple piano music. Many preschool teachers use a stringed chording instrument, such as a zither or autoharp. They are easy to play and children may " assist " the teacher with the accompaniment.

Rhythmic Experiences:

Rhythmic experiences consist of dramatizations of simple action songs, singing games, and rhythmic use of the toy instruments.

Kindergarten children can also invent new stanzas to songs and dramatize each.

Listening Experiences:

Children listen for the mood of the music, which creates the atmosphere of rest, worship, and play.

They listen to get a story from a song.

They begin to become familiar with hymns and they listen purely for enjoyment.

The piano, record player, and voice are used for listening examples.

Creative Experiences:

Preschool children can invent conversational chants and songs, one-phrase melodies, and rhythmic patterns.

Kindergarten children make simple instruments, invent instrumentation to songs and pieces, and invent new stanzas for known songs.

Primary

Singing Experiences:

Gradually the teacher can use songs that are longer and contain more ideas. One-stanza songs are best. Children enjoy sing-

ing many songs and hymns. Simple ones are best. They listen to good singing and imitate good tone.

Songs create atmosphere, attitudes, and moods, enrich the curriculum, make departmental worship meaningful, foster unity of the group, and awaken social consciousness.

Music interest groups may prepare songs for special occasions.

Children and teacher discuss the songs to be learned. The children listen several times to presentations, and learn quickly.

Primary children do not read music from hymnbooks. They learn by a simple rote method.

Songs should range between E flat (above middle C) to F in the next octave above. The high F should not be used frequently.

Playing Experiences:

The music center includes a wider variety of instruments. Not too many are available at one time.

Instruments are used in real ensemble groups.

Instruments play with the piano or record player and may be used to enrich worship services and to illustrate curriculum materials (Hebrew temple music, the psalms, etc.).

Instruments may be used to accompany songs.

A piano or an autoharp, or both, may be used for light accompaniment to the children's singing.

Rhythmic Experiences:

Song dramatizations.

Singing games. Instruments may be used.

Accompanying rhythmic movements with instruments.

Rhythmic experiences with piano and recordings, discerning the movement suggested by the music.

Processions dramatizing Hebrew festivals.

Listening Experiences:

Listening to recordings in worship services—for atmosphere.

To create attitude and moods.

To illustrate lessons.

For enjoyment.
To present artistic performances.
To learn how to listen.
To learn a hymn or song.

Creative Experiences:

Composing responses to prayer and Scripture.
Making new stanzas to known songs.
Composing tunes to Bible verses and poems.
Composing tunes to instrumental experiences.
Making instruments.

JUNIOR

Singing Experiences:

Songs are learned easily and the repertoire contains hymns, folk songs, and easy anthems.

Voices are flexible and clear.

Children like strong hymns that require emotional vitality to sing.

Folk songs are used to develop kindly attitudes toward other races and nationalities.

Hymns, responses, and anthems are sung with respectful reverence in worship services.

The children learn how to select appropriate music for worship through experience.

Songs are used to expand and enrich curriculum themes.

Special music interest groups may rehearse before the school session, or during the discovery period, in order to present music to the school groups.

Junior children may read from books while learning songs.

Some hymns and songs should be memorized.

Songs should range from middle C to F of the octave above. Because of the lowering of the voices of sixth-grade boys and the unison singing of the hymns, most of the songs should be no higher than E flat.

Playing Experiences:

Discovery groups may explore the playing of instruments, to develop curriculum materials, to play in worship and for sheer enjoyment.

Many children play the piano or other instruments well enough to play for the entire group.

Some may learn to accompany hymns.

Rhythmic Experiences:

Rhythmic experiences consist of song dramatizations, singing games, cumulative songs (weekday, vacation school, two-hour sessions) and hymn processionals.

Listening Experiences:

Listening to recordings because of the relation of the music to a study theme, to create atmosphere of worship, to learn a hymn or song, to illustrate beauty of tone and artistic performance, for enjoyment, and to teach about people of other lands, races, and cultures.

Creative Experiences:

Juniors can compose hymns — the words, tune, or both, and responses. Other creative experiences are furnished by improvised instrumental chord accompaniments for songs and instruments, and descants for hymns.

Instruments may be made and experimented with in discovery groups.

Youth

Singing Experiences:

Hymns and other songs are selected for youths taking into account the changing voice and its accompanying self-consciousness.

Youth groups provide an opportunity for informal singing experiences which encourage participation. Folk and fun songs, especially with action, secure hearty participation.

From fun songs, the transition to serious songs such as spirituals and favorite hymns is an easy and natural consequence. Plenty of hearty fellowship singing makes a singing youth department.

Fellowship books usually contain spirituals and hymns that should never be sung in the mood of fun songs.

A good youth hymnal is an essential equipment item.

A good way to teach reverent participation in worship is to teach the service music, hymns, responses, canticles, orisons, calls to worship, to the youth division. They may sing a sanctuary service for their fellowship worship and participate more fully in the congregational worship service.

The youth division will be able to learn to sing in simple two-, three-, and some four-part harmony. Unison songs should be kept in a limited middle range D to $\bar{D}$ or C to $\bar{C}$ (in some cases). It is impossible to generalize.

Playing Experiences:

Young people enjoy instrumental ensembles.

Bell ringing is an excellent activity for small groups.

Other combinations of instruments may be played together to prepare for participation in worship or fellowship events.

Young people should learn to accompany hymns. They may be used in their own age groups and in others.

Rhythmic Experiences:

Song dramatizations of folk and fun songs.

Singing games.

Cumulative songs with motions.

Folk and square dancing in fellowship events.

Listening Experiences:

Listening to recordings to study Church history, Bible stories (*Elijah, The Creation*), the life of Christ (*The Messiah, St. Matthew Passion*).

For worship services—listening for message.

To gain in sympathetic understanding of other people.

To learn the scope and significance of church music.

Listening to choirs, instruments, artists — to create interest in the profession of church music and perhaps to inspire some to choose the profession.

Creative Experiences:

Invention of harmonized arrangements of song materials, experimenting with thirds and sixths, descants, and simple pattern bass, made up of I IV V chords or scalewise, tetrachord figures.

Invention of word stanzas.

Composition of vocal or instrumental music.

Experiences with making instruments in the musical laboratory or workshop.

Chapter 11

PLANNING FOR THE MUSIC PROGRAM OF THE CHURCH

CHURCHES of all sizes and kinds that use any music need to study to integrate it into their programs and to use to the best advantage all available resources. Many churches, especially new ones and those which are growing rapidly in congregation and activities, have poorly integrated music programs. The size of the professional staff has not increased in proportion to their need, and there is insufficient leadership for any music other than the choir program. A leader, trained both in Christian education and in music, is needed to help organize and develop an educational program, but there are still very few churches in the country that provide professional staff members for this purpose. Small churches are inclined to regard the mediocre as inevitable and to make little or no attempt to improve or extend their programs.

The question arises as to whose responsibility it is to plan and administer a music education program in the church. Most churches have a music committee, and this committee has an important function to perform. Looking to the minister and the director of music for guidance, the committee should examine and evaluate the musical activities of its organizations in order to determine the adequacy of the total music program of the church. Then it should assume leadership in planning for and implementing an expanded use of music in the total church program.

The membership of the committee should include representa-

tives from the central governing board of the church, the church school staff, parents of choir children, parents of youth, the adult organizations, the adult choir, the Christian education committee. In very small churches there might be no children's or youth choirs to be represented.

The music of the church should be evaluated according to the effectiveness with which it is being used in the entire church program for the purposes of enriching worship and teaching the faith. Answers to the following questions should be sought by the committee:

1. Does the music in the church worship services lift the spirit of the congregation to a high level of worship?

2. Is the music of such a character that it does not interrupt the "flow" of the service by attracting attention to itself?

3. Does the congregation participate well in the music of the services?

4. Are unfamiliar hymns introduced frequently? Does the congregation accept them?

5. Is the quality of the music that is used in all the organizations of the church on a high aesthetic level, or is there a double standard for music in the church? Is the denominational hymnal used in the church sanctuary and a book of choruses or gospel hymns in the Sunday church school?

6. Who decides what songbooks or hymnals shall be purchased for use in the Sunday church school classes (including the adult classes)?

7. Who is responsible for co-ordinating and unifying the course of study in church music in the church? Are there learning experiences in music provided for the entire congregation? No matter how small the church, some teaching may be provided.

8. Are there choirs for children and youths as well as adults?

9. Will the music budget meet the demands of the growing program?

10. Is music used in the teaching program of the church school, and is it well integrated into the curriculum?

There are three approaches to the program of the church, and

music can make an important contribution to all of them. The committee should plan consistently for them.

1. *The program areas* may be classified as (*a*) Faith, (*b*) Witness, (*c*) Evangelism and Stewardship, (*d*) Fellowship, and (*e*) World Mission. In each of these areas music can greatly accent the program emphasis.

2. *The curriculum of the school* can be greatly enriched by related music. Hymns and songs and recorded materials are available to be used at the different age levels, to illuminate the study of the life of Jesus Christ, the Bible, and the Church. Listings of both songs and recordings and the age to which they are best suited will be found in Chapters 5, 8, and 10 of this book.

3. *The age levels of the entire family* should be considered in the music plans for the church.

The music committee, in assuming responsibility for the music of the church, must find a way to provide an adequate leadership and plan for accomplishing its purposes. Responsibility for the music of the church should lead the committee to think creatively of the possible improvements of the existing music program and of providing needed new expressional outlets and equipment. The following possibilities should be explored by the committee, and incorporated into the church, with consideration of its size:

1. In the Sunday church school training should be provided for the superintendents and teachers, in the purposes of church music; they should be taught how to select appropriate music; if possible, a musician, probably the choir director, should be invited to attend the departmental planning sessions to assist in integrating music into the lesson plans and to suggest music that will enrich the study themes, as well as to show how to present and teach music; suggestions should be made of imaginative ways to stimulate interest in good music; the teachers' own level of appreciation should be raised; accompanists and leaders for special projects should be supplied. Where a music educator is not available, a group study of Chapters 1, 10, and 12 of this book should prove helpful to the church school staff.

2. The organizations of the church should be helped to discover and secure musical talent for leading and accompanying hymn and fellowship singing, and to develop imagination in the use of music in their program areas. One such program in the area of missionary education, which I heard many years ago, made a lasting impression on me.

Dr. Bliss Wiant, who had taught music for many years in Yenching University in Peiping, came to the First Methodist Church in Hackensack, New Jersey, bringing his instruments and a rich store of stories which he told with a charm which makes him fascinating to children and adults alike. He presented a program on Chinese music in which the audience participated by singing some of the Chinese songs that he had collected, arranged, and published. Interspersed with the music was Dr. Wiant's story of Christian missions in China. I have heard many impressive missionary programs, but never one that I have remembered more vividly and pleasantly.

Most of the missionary materials published by Friendship Press contain, in the leader's guides, ideas for the use of music. *The Whole World Singing,* by Edith Lovell Thomas, contains folk songs from around the world. The Fun and Festival Series contains folk songs of the nations. These materials, along with recorded folk music, will enable small churches to relate music, with imagination, to the missionary themes.

3. Special educational opportunities in music should be planned for. An informal course in hymnology given at a series of Family Nights noticeably improved the congregational hymn singing in one congregation. A young people's group that studied the use of music in worship greatly improved the quality of its worship services. The children in a junior department studied the hymnal and created their own hymns, thereby increasing their joy in participation in hymn singing. By careful planning, such benefits could be extended to reach the entire congregation. The music of the Bible, the life of Jesus in music, the history of the Church through the hymnal are some of the very many special studies that are helpful. These are available to the small, as well as the

large congregations. Visiting lecturers and artists, vesper services developed on special themes, and choir festivals, are all inspirational and educational ways to extend musical education in the church.

4. There should be a long-range plan for the provision of musical organizations that are needed to meet the needs of the church. Where there is a full program in music, demanding time and professional leadership, the committee will need to recommend the securing of a person to direct the program. For the sake of unity in the music program, it is advisable to have one person to head the ministry of music. Some churches solve their leadership problems by using several local musicians on a part-time basis. Such an arrangement is less likely to be satisfactory, partly because of the lack of unity in purpose and plan, and partly because of personality difficulties which result from divided authority. Part-time employees are less likely to have had professional training in the administration of a program in church music.

Recommendations for a long-range program should be based upon the needs of the church, its probable ability to support the program, and the stability of a staff to develop a program and stay with it until it is on a secure footing.

Some of the musical organizations that have proved valuable in other churches should be evaluated in the light of their practicability and usefulness in the present situation. The following items should be considered:

1. Singing choirs can be made to appeal to all age levels, and opportunities may be provided for regular participation of all choirs in church worship services. Some churches provide, in addition to choirs, classes in sight reading and ear training.

2. Instrumental ensembles are gaining in popularity. English hand bells were introduced to American churches by Dr. and Mrs. Clarence Dickinson, who brought a set from England to the Brick Presbyterian Church in New York City. Rev. Donald Kettring has organized an ensemble of orchestral instruments in the East Liberty Presbyterian Church of Pittsburgh, for the

purpose, primarily, of accompanying the singing choirs in special services.

3. Choir camps and music workshops are highly recommended items in the program of music.

A choir camp provides an excellent opportunity to integrate musical experience into the daily routine of Christian living. Plenty of shared fun, fellowship, out-of-doors activities, and music make a choir camp a valuable contribution to Christian education. Every song learned at camp is especially beloved because of the memory associations. The carry-over that comes from daily rehearsals far exceeds that which derives from the same number of weekly rehearsals during the school year. The warm personal contacts that are possible in a camp bring director and singers into a relationship that is reflected in the music thereafter.

4. A music workshop for teachers and leaders of music in the church is a valuable addition to the program. Young people and adults can learn the use of music in worship, the correct use of the voice, and how to teach and lead music. If local professional leadership for the workshop is not obtainable, many denominations can supply leadership to their churches. Books and pamphlets may be studied by an apt leader and a workshop guided by nonprofessional leadership. See the Bibliography in this book for suggestions.

Summer training schools in the leadership of church music are held in all areas of the country. Some are supported by denominations. Others are nondenominational. The cost of attendance is, in some cases, little more than the cost of board and room. The benefit that is carried back to a church is amazing. Few churches that need professional help can honestly afford to neglect this kind of expenditure for their employed or volunteer musicians.

5. Adequate equipment must be provided and kept in repair. At the top of the list is, of course, the pipe organ, which beautifies the church worship services. Regular maintenance is necessary to keep it in good condition. In addition, some or all of the following items should be added, according to the church's needs

and budget—pianos (kept in tune), record player and records, tape recorder, hymnals and fellowship songbooks, a reference library on music, a library of anthems, and robes for the choirs. The English hand bells are a lovely addition. Toy rhythm instruments for little children are important.

6. Publicity and promotion are vital to undergird the music program. The committee members should assume the responsibility for this, for they are best qualified to educate the people on the quality and value of their music program. It is a joy to see a committee do a really effective job in making a congregation aware of its obligation to support the efforts of the choirs and directors.

7. Planning and administering the music budget will require a considerable amount of study. In addition to providing equipment, at least some of the following items are to be considered: salaries of organist, director, soloists, special artists; fellowship expenditures such as picnics and parties, choir camps, workshops and conferences; robes; printed brochures and programs; and educational advantages for directors, including expenses to conventions, workshops, and summer training schools.

The most important thing to remember is that program and equipment do not necessarily make effective Christian education. Music is *Christian* education only when it leads to a warm relationship with God through Jesus Christ. This can be done simply and effectively in a one-room church with a small budget if the standards are high, or it can fail miserably in a large "important" church that puts its major emphasis on organizations and equipment. It is what happens to people as individuals in a group that matters, and the best tools in the world cannot substitute for Christian warmth and enthusiasm. A music committee of a very small church may be led, through its study and evaluation, to carry on an educational program in music that will lift the music spiritually and aesthetically to a high level of worship and education. A large church may find that it needs to expand staff, add equipment, and project a planned program

into the future that will reach all of the congregation at all age levels, in all program areas, and offer more expressional outlets for more people. Whatever it concludes it must do, at least the committee should have a plan, and custom-build the program to the needs of the church.

Chapter 12

OBJECTIVES AND STANDARDS FOR MUSIC IN CHRISTIAN EDUCATION

A CHRISTIAN education program furnishes the atmosphere, experiences, and training that should lead to the acceptance of Christ as the Lord of Life and should foster continual Christian growth. A well-administered program of Christian music should also do this, and if it does, it is, to a high degree, Christian education. Because music has the power to raise the level of religious experience, Christian education should be tremendously concerned over the inclusion and integration, in the curriculum, of the most carefully selected music.

As suggested in Chapter 1, some of the objectives of Christian education are better achieved through the use of music than by any of the other teaching media. In planning for the most effective use of music in a curriculum, the educator should first clearly define the purposes of Christian teaching, and, in the light of the growth stage of the pupils, determine what procedures and what music will best enrich the curriculum. Satisfactory integration cannot be accomplished unless we start with basic aims. The Division of Christian Education of the National Council of Churches has made a concise chart of objectives on the age levels. There is also an unusually helpful little pamphlet, *Your Child Grows Toward God,* by Pearl Rosser (The Judson Press), which tabulates the growth stages in Christian development.

A starting point in planning for the integration of music into the Christian education program should be the definition of the

Christian goals and a graded plan for their achievement in harmony with the capacities of the age levels.

While some music appeals to and has meaning for all ages of people, much of it is more useful at specific age levels than at others. This is the reason that graded hymnals are an important part of a church school curriculum. The task of selection of hymns has been partially eliminated with the choice of good graded hymnals. They are as important to good teaching as are other graded curriculum materials. This is not a denial of the fact that there should be a body of hymn material that can be used effectively by groups of mixed ages, even though all the words cannot be explained to the youngest children for immediate complete understanding. Some songs should be regarded as "songs to grow on," and should be included in the church family repertoire for the purposes of Christian fellowship. A list of these hymns is included in the chapter on hymns.

If music is to be related to all of a child's life, and continue to be so, as the child grows, then Christian educators must learn to make intelligent selections of music on the basis of:

1. The goals of Christian education.
2. The age level characteristics — mental, emotional, spiritual.
3. The musical capacity of the age levels.
4. The worth of the music.
5. The ability of the music to communicate to the age level.

To like a piece of music is not sufficient reason in itself for its inclusion in a curriciulum. Musical taste may have been immature when the liking was acquired. Enthusiasm for the song will be communicated to those who are taught. Perhaps the song is not worthy of perpetuation. On the other hand, the song may be excellent, but unsuited to the use to be made of it. The following standards will serve as criteria in the selection of songs:

1. The ideas in the songs should be in harmony with the total curriculum. Right ideas of God, Jesus, the Bible, the Church and social relationships must be embodied in the songs. Take, for

example, the idea that one can pray at any time and anywhere, which is well expressed in the song "I Talk to God Wherever I May Be" (*Hymns for Primary Worship,* No. 38):

"I talk to God wherever I may be,
At school, at home, at church, or at my play;
He understands the thoughts I try to say —
He hears me! God hears me!

"I talk to God when I am very glad
For lovely things that happen every day;
I tell Him "thank you" in my own small way —
He hears me! God hears me!

"I talk to God when I am ill or sad;
I whisper to Him when I feel afraid;
He helps me to do right when I have prayed —
God hears me! God hears me!"

— *Kathryn Blackburn Peck.*

2. The song-poem should be well-expressed and the phraseology suited to the age level for which it is intended. Sometimes simple ideas are expressed in phrases that need a great deal of explanation, and sometimes ideas phrased in simple words are too deep for children to comprehend. Although it is easier to explain words than ideas, it is well for both to have meaning for the singers. Symbolism is inappropriate to use with young children. For example, the poetic beauty of Psalm 104, paraphrased by Robert Grant in "O Worship the King" will be lost to children whose limited experience would prevent them from interpreting the word pictures with any real meaning. Even for junior children the poem is too heavily symbolic. The hymn becomes useful for juniors with careful editing. Three stanzas, the first, second, and third, set to the appropriate tune arranged from J. Michael Haydn, make this good hymn suitable to use with junior children.

"All Glory, Laud, and Honor" (Theodulph of Orleans), which is sung on Palm Sunday in all our churches, contains words

like "laud," "Redeemer," "hosannas," which are not in the conversational vocabulary of primary children. Nevertheless, the concepts are easily grasped through simple explanation, and the song is given meaningful usage. The literary value is important. Eternal truths, God's laws for the universe and for our lives, should be spoken of in language of beauty and sincerity, the language of good poetry. Consider, as an example, this simple, direct song text from *Hymns for Primary Worship,* No. 15:

> "O God, whose laws will never change,
> We thank You for these things we know:
> That after rain the sun will shine;
> That after darkness light appears;
> That winter always brings the spring;
> That after sleep we wake again;
> That life goes on, and love remains,
> And life and love can never die."
>
> —*Jeanette E. Perkins. Copyright, The Pilgrim Press. Used by permission.*

3. The rhythmic framework of the song should be strong. Rhythm furnishes the structural balance and proportion of music. All markedly rhythmic music is not necessarily in good rhythm. Clapping a rhythm will sometimes help to evaluate it. Monotonous repetition of a dotted eighth or sixteenth note figure tends to cheapen composition. Julia Ward Howe's "Battle Hymn of the Republic" has survived, in magnificent grandeur, in spite of the trite rhythm with which it has been associated. One has only to tap out the rhythm to see what the effect would be without the benefit of the beautiful words. One should beware of all "jingly" rhythms. Songs with repeated syncopations, the kind that affect the feet primarily, are not good for religious expression. For example, the accenting of the second pulse throughout will give this effect:

4/4 ♩ 𝅗𝅥 ♩ | ♩ 𝅗𝅥 ♩ | ♩ 𝅗𝅥 ♩ | 𝅝 ||

Contrast with that "limping" rhythm the strongly marked one of the "Adeste Fideles," which also employs a $\frac{4}{4}$ framework, but has majesty and spirit in the distribution of accents:

$\frac{4}{4}$ ♩ | 𝅗𝅥 ♩ ♩ | 𝅗𝅥 ♩ ♩ | ♩ ♩ ♩ ♩ | 𝅗𝅥 ♩ ‖

4. Simple melodic lines are more apt to be good than over-elaborate ones. The tune should be singable and in the same spirit as the words. "Fairest Lord Jesus" is an excellent example of a well-formed tune. It lies almost entirely within an octave range, moves diatonically with few intervals larger than a third. The graceful dignity of the song-poem is repeated in the tune. Words and music communicate the same idea. The melody of a song becomes so completely linked with the words that it becomes difficult to disassociate them in one's thoughts. For this reason alone a good melody is of great importance.

"Melody streams from the heart flowing upon the joyous impulses of the soul in tune and in time with Infinite Cause.

"Melody is the charted movement of the feelings made glad by the soul's approval. In its harmonious embrace, brief as it may be, we feel related to something somewhere beyond ourselves" (*Beyond the Tonal Horizon of Music,* by Frederick Schlieder).

5. Harmonic value is difficult for the musically uneducated to judge. There are basic laws governing harmonization which, if followed, give a satisfactory effect. Harmony is inherent in the structure of a melody. It is also obvious when two or more parts appear simultaneously. Harmony enters into vocal music through the part song or by way of instrumental accompaniment to melody. For the purpose of accompanying children's voices, the harmonization should be simple, unobtrusive, and primary. Songs for the very young are effective without harmonization. In the youth and adult divisions of the church, two-, three-, and four-part music may be sung without difficulty. The hymns in their hymnals are usually written in harmonized form. Good harmonizations enrich the meaning of the texts. An example of a very good harmonization in a hymn is "St. Anne," by William

Croft. Isaac Watts's words "Our God, Our Help in Ages Past" are at one with the strong harmony of the music.

Having said all of this in classes for many years, and having used examples both good and not so good, I am no longer surprised to have people come to me after a session concentrated on evaluation and selection, hand me a book of choruses or a book of gospel hymns, and ask seriously of specific hymns, "Isn't this good music?" Because our taste is something about which we are all more or less sensitive, it is difficult to discuss the subject and not tread on feelings. And the sensitivity is more acute when the experience association with the hymn is strong and important. The important factor is not that leaders should destroy experience memories, but that they must recognize the inadvisability of perpetuating unsuitable music with those to whom they teach music for its teaching value.

We do not necessarily recognize beauty because we have been told that it exists. The degree to which we discern beauty is, to some extent, determined by the experience that we have had with it, just as we cannot fully comprehend goodness until we have seen pure goodness in Jesus Christ. Mrs. Clarence Dickinson tells a story about an encounter that a Brooklyn librarian had with some young apartment house dwellers. Passing down a street paved with cement from one side to the other, she came upon a little group of children looking intently at something in the center of their closed circle. Recognizing some of the children, she asked what it was at which they were gazing. Whereupon, they faced her with glowing faces and pointed to a crack in the cement in which was growing a tiny patch of grass. "Look, Miss Brown," they cried, "it's a park." Souls starved for musical expression, and never having learned to discriminate between true beauty and its poor imitation, sometimes eagerly accept songs that have no more in common with true hymns than the patch of grass had with a real park.

"Without discrimination it is impossible to recognize even the crude materials of music, for the first step is already a coordination of these materials." (H. E. Krehbiel, *How to Listen to Music,* pp. 16, 17.)

Chapter 13

MUSIC IN THE CHURCH PROGRAM AREAS

THE CHURCH program covers four major areas or emphases that are touched to some extent in each age level: Faith, Witness, Outreach, and Fellowship. To each of these areas music can make a significant contribution, and is, perhaps, the most potent of all the ways in which we carry on the program of Christian education in these areas.

Faith in Jesus Christ is the reason for the existence of his Church and the foundation of all of its life and growth. Christian faith must be cultivated and helped to grow. In order to have a vital, forceful Christian experience, we must relate our faith to the whole of life.

The church seeks to lead people to find and develop a Christian faith through worship, study, and action. One of the most effective and sound ways for men to strengthen their faith is to study what God has said to men down through the ages. The most outstanding record we have of God's speaking to men is found in the Bible, and to read and study it can have the most deepening influence on the spiritual life.

God has spoken to and through men of all ages and in many ways. "The Bible is a living record of man's search for God. But that record stopped short nearly two thousand years ago. Today the hymnbook is the best contemporary recording of great religious experience that we have. It bridges the centuries from Bible times to this day, and lifts from the stream of life the poetic aspirations and the singing hopes that have sustained and

strengthened the greatest and humblest men." (*Guideposts to Creative Family Worship,* Edward W. and Anna L. Gebhard, p. 67; Abingdon Press, 1953; used by permission.) Next to the Bible, the hymns of the faith have had the greatest influence on the spiritual life of people. The Bible and the hymnal stand together as witnesses to God's continued communication with men. It is hard to understand how Christians can sing great hymns in a careless, lifeless manner, or resort to cheap, sentimental substitutes for the virile expressions of faith in our good hymns. Ecstatic religious experiences have found their greatest expression in the creation of hymns. Less creative souls have used these hymns to strengthen and express their faith. The church that recognizes the potency of the hymn in the strengthening of faith will include in its program opportunities for the people to grow in their appreciation and ability to use them. A separate chapter has been devoted to further discussion of the significance of the study of hymns in the church.

Christians should have two great objectives: to know Jesus Christ and to make him known. The possession of Christian faith carries with it the responsibility to witness for him; to share our time, talents, and lives. In this area of the church program, music is one which most challenges Christian stewardship. Most churches greatly need people to serve in a musical capacity and to help beautify the services. Volunteer choirs can achieve their purposes only when singers who are faithful in fulfilling their obligation fill the ranks. Pianists are needed for church school departments and organizational meetings. A well-filled choir loft, good pianists in church school departments, and hearty congregational singing all bear witness to the faith we have in Jesus Christ. The witness of a dedicated musician can bear much fruit.

> "Take my life, and let it be
> Consecrated, Lord, to Thee.
> Take my moments and my days;
> Let them flow in ceaseless praise."
> —*Frances Ridley Havergal.*

This should be the sincere prayer of the choir singers. When it is, people will be drawn to worship services and, perhaps, to Christ and church membership through the music. Great religious leaders have recognized the power of music in evangelization. Choirs have always been a strong force for evangelization. This is such an important function of the choir that there should be a plan for recruitment, follow-up on members, and choir promotion that is carried on by music committees and other organizations of the church. In too many churches, this important task is left entirely to the organist-director, who rarely ever has the contacts to work at the task efficiently by himself. Churches must become aware of the fact that the choir is the concern of the entire congregation.

Missions of love and service can be performed by Christian musicians. There are shut-ins who enjoy hearing tape recordings of the music of the church. People in homes for the aged and other institutions enjoy being entertained by musical groups from the churches. Youth choirs, bell choirs, and soloists are always welcomed guests where there are people who cannot attend church.

Jesus said, "Go therefore and make disciples of all nations" (Matt. 28:19). Jesus obviously meant for us to share the gospel with the whole world. Although our music will not be apt to take us literally into the whole world, it can help us to build our world outlook and outreach as we grow in our own faith. Through music we can learn the meaning of:

> "O brother man, fold to thy heart thy brother;
> Where pity dwells, the peace of God is there;
> To worship rightly is to love each other,
> Each smile a hymn, each kindly deed a prayer."
> —*John Greenleaf Whittier.*

Through their music we become sympathetic and more understanding of other nations and races. There are hymns in the hymnals that represent different countries and races and can be used with explanations of the reasons for their use. Folk songs

help us to know people better. They will enrich the study of friendship frontiers and mission study books. Although we may not go ourselves to carry the gospel, by our loving understanding we may create an atmosphere in which someone else may find that his vocation is to serve Christ through music.

People of all ages, joined in Christian fellowship, form the church family. As they share in worship, service, and recreation, they draw closer to one another. Christian living is a shared experience. Christian faith is strengthened and enriched through Christian fellowship. Music contributes to Christian fellowship in the home, the church, and the wider community. The church can demonstrate to families the ways by which music can draw them more closely together in Christian fellowship at home: through Family Night gatherings where there is informal singing of folk songs, hymns, and fun songs; through recommendation of records and demonstration of their use for family listening; through family hymn festivals. The radio, television, and record player have made it possible to bring into our homes artists' performances of beautiful music. Before the advent of these mechanical devices, families and social groups used to make their own music, gathering informally around a piano to sing, or to play instruments. There are still families who enjoy the close fellowship that comes from singing or playing together, but the vast majority have no idea of the family unity that could be the result of such an experience. Gathering as a family to sing hymns and folk tunes is one of the happiest memories of my childhood. Mother played the piano, and sang alto, Father led with a hearty intermittent bass or tenor, and the children sang soprano or alto depending on their ages. Mother knew the names of all the tunes in the hymnal and could play them. Father knew the great hymn-poems from memory and could recite them. My first association with many hymns came in this way. "Once to every man and nation comes the moment to decide" will always be associated in my mind with my father's dramatic voice. The strength of moral decision was thundered in these words as they rang from his bedroom, where he always recited hymns while he

dressed. "Our God, our Help in ages past, our Hope for years to come" seemed to be a family favorite, for I recall singing it so frequently that the words fell naturally from my lips at an early age. The family that does not sing hymns together misses one of the greatest bonds of Christian fellowship and spiritual devotion in the home.

The Christian church has a responsibility for helping families to discover and use ways to make warmer and more secure the foundations of Christian fellowship. The Family Night plan of the church program can be used to show the way. At one such program for families, when the group sang hymns a three-year-old child who was sitting on his mother's lap looked knowingly at his songbook and sang unrestrainedly any words he could think of. He was truly "making a joyful noise unto the Lord" and sharing in a real sense the warm fellowship created through the music. When there is free choice of the music to be sung, the children are usually the first to make requests. Folk song collections are a good investment for churches. All organizations have times when singing folk songs will add to their fun and fellowship. Fun songs learned at the church have a way of insinuating themselves into family life. If the entire family learns them at a Family Night, they are almost certain to crop up at such times as riding in the car, doing dishes together, and at other tasks. In lieu of the song collection for each singer, song slides or song charts with words hand-printed in large letters will suffice for learning the songs.

A family hymn festival brings together families for the purpose of singing hymns. Special days and occasions give impetus to this type of event. Thanksgiving, Christmas, Easter, a birthday of a great hymn writer, anniversaries of great events, such as the printing of the Genevan Psalter, all can and have been celebrated with a family hymn festival. The most popular and frequently repeated festival is held at Christmas time when families gather at the church to sing carols and hymns. Most churches have their own version of this event. People so enjoy it that it is a wonder that more churches do not plan to have similar celebrations for

other special days in the Church year.

We need not relegate the mechanical musical instrument to a position of disfavor in regard to Christian unity of the family. There are many excellent recordings of beautiful religious music which families could learn to enjoy together. There is a unity which comes from listening to music and enjoying it together. Here, again, the way can be demonstrated by playing at the church some beautiful recorded music, and by teaching families how to listen together for specific spots in the music.

A list of records for family use, as well as for special age levels, is included in the chapter on recorded music. A church director can mimeograph a list of his own record recommendations to be sent into the homes.

In every organization of the church, whenever people meet together, music has a contribution to make. Youth groups, adult groups, Women's Association meetings, men's clubs, congregational meetings, family gatherings—all can use music to foster fellowship, to strengthen faith, to witness through service, and to extend outreach, for music is related to all of life.

Choirs are wonderful organizations for fostering Christian fellowship. People who sing together are not strangers, even though the choir is their only place of contact. When calls are made on prospective new members of the church, one of the important questions should be, "Do you sing?" A new member who joins one of the choirs is drawn at once into the warm fellowship of service. Regular church attendance and vital interest resulting from participation in the program help make good church members.

The reader's inventiveness will lead him to add many more creative techniques and plans for the use of music to achieve the purpose of the total church program through its program areas.

Chapter 14

CHOIRS AND THE CHOIR DIRECTOR

THE PURPOSES and functions of church choirs in the Protestant churches are essentially the same regardless of size, budget, and location. Systems may be as far apart as the poles; program and activities may range from exceedingly simple to most elaborate, but they all exist for the same reasons.

Recent statistics have revealed that the average Protestant church in America has two hundred and fifty members and carries on its program with little equipment and with only one full-time member of the staff, a minister. The sexton and the organist-choir director are both part-time employees. Some of these part-time church musicians have had a thorough musical education which helps them to gain the respect of their choir members. Some have read and studied or even attended summer choir schools to gain Christian purpose, choral techniques, and repertoire. However, in many cases the choir director has made no study of church music, its purposes, its hymn literature, or its anthem repertoire. The adult choir is a struggling, irregular organization, and the children's choir, if there is one, reflects the insecurity of the poorly prepared director.

Fortunately the understanding and appreciation of music and the ability to produce good choir music does not depend on the size of the church or the choir. Any church that has a minister who is aware of the true value of choirs and their purposes, and who is eager to lift the spiritual and aesthetic level of his congregation, through music, can find the way to improvement. If

his seminary training did not include a course in hymnology, he can start his efforts to improve the situation by getting a book such as *Lyric Religion,* by H. Augustine Smith, and study in order to stimulate the choir and the congregation to greater interest and appreciation of hymns. If there is a potential choir leader in the congregation or community, the minister can encourage him to read such books as *Music in Worship,* by Walter S. Swisher; *Church Music in History and Practice,* by Winfred Douglas; *Lyric Religion,* by H. Augustine Smith; *The Successful Children's Choir,* by Ruth Krehbiel Jacobs; and *Music and Worship,* A Manual for the Organist and the Choir Director, by Federal Lee Whittlesey. The potential leader should be sent, if possible, to a one or two weeks' summer choir school. The organization of a children's choir will help to secure the future of the music in the small church.

The size of the choir does not exclude the use of music of high value. Many simple unison anthems have real beauty. Hymns from the denominational hymnal may be used as anthems, and interpreted in artistic style by choirs of any number of people. They may be sung in unison or four-part harmony. There are also hymn anthems available in one-, two-, and four-part arrangements. Some of these are given in the anthem lists of this book. The soprano, alto, baritone arrangements suggested elsewhere are usable with small adult choirs, even choirs that have only one or two men.

This section on church choirs is written in an attempt to be helpful to churches of all sizes with any number of choirs. Many things apply to all. Many of the suggestions are in the nature of "choir education at the goal" and all choirs will need to stretch up to achieve them. Whether you have one choir or six, the same purposes, principles of education, ways of learning, rehearsing, and singing hold good; the same standards for music are valid, and the same Christian discipline is needed. The minister and the choir director of a church with two hundred and fifty or less members can strive for and achieve a good choir.

Choirs have inherited their high office in the service of the

church from tradition that dates back to the ordination, by David, of the sons of Levi: "These are the men whom David put in charge of the service of song in the house of the Lord, after the ark rested there. They ministered with song before the tabernacle of the tent of meeting, until Solomon had built the house of the Lord in Jerusalem: and they performed their service in due order." (I Chron. 6:31, 32.) The choir members were ordained to serve the Lord with song and were assigned a place to live.

The Roman Church continued the tradition of special regard for the status of choir singers. The medieval church had choir schools where boys were trained in the music of the church and served the church in the choir. There are some few choir schools in America today, in the Roman Catholic and Episcopal Churches, which exist for the dual purpose of Christian training through music and providing music for the church. They are specialized parochial schools.

In the Protestant churches the office of the choir is regarded in a variety of ways. Unfortunately some choirs have failed to live up to their high calling, have fallen into disrepute, and have been dropped from the church entirely. Some people hold the extreme view that the choir exists for the purpose of brightening an otherwise drab service, with entertainment. At the opposite extreme are the choirs to whom the response of the congregation is of no concern and who overly emphasize the liturgical function. In between these extreme attitudes are the many churches that regard the choir as a group set apart, because of their special musical aptitude, to lead the congregation in worship.

The choir is a group set apart because of its musical ability and high purposes to serve God in his church. Choirs learn reverence in worship, service to the church, regular church attendance, Christian fellowship—group expression, beautiful religious music, vocal skills, music fundamentals.

Children's choirs will make sure the foundations for the adult choir of the future.

The main functions of the choir are related to the church wor-

ship services. H. Augustine Smith in the chapter "The Expression of Religion in Music" states that church musicians serve best in the church:

"1. Through singing *with* the congregation on hymns, chants, responses, and through leading in responsive readings and attitudes of prayer. . . . The choirs thus supply tonal, rhythmical, intellectual, and spiritual guidance.

"2. Through singing *for* the congregation. Here the people, unable to join in the higher art form of anthem, chorale, and short motet, sing silently, while choristers voice prayer and praise, yearnings and ecstasies. For this vicarious act, singers should take vows of chastity, humility, and dedication, for only those of clean hands and pure hearts may rightly lift to the throne of grace the petitions and thanksgiving of a worshiping people.

"3. Through singing *to* the congregation, the choir renders a personal service as comforter and exhorter to each and every layman. Thus music is no longer a profession, but a principle, with the singer an evangelist, with discerning instinct, and sustained fervor, imparting his faith to others." (*The Arts and Religion,* edited by Albert E. Bailey, p. 118.)

In fulfilling these functions, a choir acts as a deputy for the minister. Robert B. Lee, in an article entitled "The Sacrament of Music," said: "When he rises to sing the anthem, each choir member is charged with the responsibility of bringing to the assembled congregation music of dynamic religious power. At this point the well-trained choir reaches a power of religious experience as great as the sermon itself." For this "each chorister must necessarily dedicate himself to the glorification of God and man, as he is the manifestation of that glory." (*Union Seminary Quarterly Review,* January, 1949, p. 20.)

Early in the eighteenth century, a Moravian hymn writer who was destined to have a vital influence on John Wesley, the founder of Methodism, Count Von Zinzendorf, compiled a hymnal which he used particularly with children, for the purpose of Christian education. He organized his followers into an

elaborate system of small bands, according to age, sex, and marital status, for the purpose of worship and discussion. These bands, called "choirs," often sang in their group meetings and together in song services.

The multiple choir system is gaining in popularity in America. Even small churches have two choirs, an adult and a children's choir. Larger churches have up to five or six choirs. Whether a church takes the high view expressed by Robert B. Lee that a choir can reach "a power of religious experience as great as the sermon," or the somewhat lower view that the choir is an attraction to draw a crowd, it will have to agree that a choir is a powerful instrument and as such may not be disregarded.

Churches that cannot have the professional leadership of a trained church musician have two or three courses open to them in organizing a choir or improving an existing choir organization. There are situations in which the minister is the only person in the parish who has the background required to start the choir program. He is a busy man and should not actually have to direct the choir. Through his enthusiasm, knowledge of resources and of leadership technique and purposes of choirs, he may encourage, advise, and guide someone else to do a creditable job and to develop in it. Sometimes the minister actually has to direct the choir himself if there is to be one. In any event he should study to improve himself and to discover and train leadership. If there are any funds available, the church should invest in the future by sending one or two people away for short terms to study church music.

Some churches have to rely completely on nonprofessional or semiprofessional leadership for choirs. In many towns and cities the directors are selected because they have had some music lessons, either instrumental, vocal, or both. Other churches need and are able to employ church musicians, and are not completely sure about the necessary qualifications.

An ideal choir director has certain characteristics which exist in various degrees of attainment and maturity. Choir directors may take their own measure by this list:

1. A choir director should first of all be a Christian with a warm personality to which people respond and which they are willing to follow. He is sincere, loyal, and dependable. In the chapter on Christian discipline this is more thoroughly discussed.

2. A choir director is a church musician and must have certain basic qualifications. Natural musical ability is the base of musicianship, but only the accepted starting point, for ability must be developed and trained before it can be used with authority and skill. The more study and education the better, but there are a few branches more fundamentally important than others: a knowledge of the fundamentals of melody, scales, keys, rhythm, and measure; ear training, and sight reading; basic harmony; fundamentals of conducting, and laws of interpretation.

3. A choir director needs some musical skills. He should know how to sing, producing tone correctly, and be able to discern the fine degrees of differences in tone in other voices. Some keyboard facility is necessary, enough for working out new music.

4. A choir director should know the relationship of church music to worship.

5. A choir director should know hymns and hymnology.

6. A choir director should be conversant with standard choral repertoire, and know standards for selection.

This list of requirements is not intended to frighten a beginning choir director, but to suggest the direction that his musical study should take. As an educator, the choir director should be conversant with the principles of education and psychology as they apply to religion and to music. He should know these laws of learning and how to apply them. They are the law of readiness, the law of effect, and the law of use.

A choir director should take time to motivate his teaching and prepare his singers for learning a song. Unless they wish to learn, their response will be halfhearted, and the teaching time lengthened. The effect of teaching under pleasant circumstances is positive and more permanent. However, the acquired knowledge has to be used, or it will be easily lost. The Chinese use a proverb, "Unused knowledge quickly vanishes away."

People learn best by their own experiences. The creative choir director makes sure that the singer's own ingenuity and initiative are put to work in the learning procedure to avoid a parrotlike process which has little value in teaching.

People learn by imitation and example. This is really an indirect kind of teaching and learning, to which the teacher rarely calls attention.

People learn by repetition. A good teacher finds new approaches to repetition. Each time a song is brought out for rehearsal some new point of interest is discovered or an old one recalled and refreshed, thus reviving enthusiasm which might otherwise lag.

People learn by the association of new ideas and information with familiar ones.

Satisfaction must be gained from the learning effort. People must be helped to feel that they have achieved. Music gives the learner a tremendous sense of satisfaction, because the entire person — mind, body, emotions, and spirit — has contributed to the process. The choir director should always remember this and plan deliberately, so that each rehearsal and each performance will leave the singers with a sense of accomplishment.

A choir director should study with care the characteristics of the ages with which he is working. Books written for secular education and for Christian educators are listed in the Bibliography. Accepting a person where he is, loving him, and helping him to grow through shared experiences with music is an exciting adventure. When a choir director stops " teaching music " and begins to " share his music " with people, he and they relax and enjoy it.

Chapter 15

CHRISTIAN DISCIPLINE AND CHURCH CHOIRS

A CHOIR director, whether he knows it or not, is a Christian educator, dealing with one of the most potent instruments of Christian education — music. For this responsibility, the most important personal equipment he has is his *Christian* personality. Except for this one quality, the personal qualifications for a choir director and for any choral director are the same, but this one quality makes all the difference in the world. It qualifies and affects his total plan and work. It is not enough to say that it is required that he "be a Christian," for too frequently the term is misused to refer to anyone who professes belief in Christ and joins a church, whether or not he acts according to his belief.

To Jesus' disciples, and to the early Christians, it was a costly thing to be a Christian. The term implied the practice of a discipline, freely accepted, as followers of Jesus. Jesus' disciples taught by example and instruction in order that the good news might be spread, and the Kingdom of love might come.

To be a true Christian still costs in sacrifice and service, and requires the practice of discipline. We cannot teach Christianity without teaching Christian discipline, nor can we teach what we do not practice. Because too often there exist great discrepancies between Christian belief and the popular conception of the meaning of discipline as it applies to the control of groups, it seems wise to elaborate in more detail on the fact that the practices of group leadership in a choir rehearsal should be consistent with Christian personality. It is a generally accepted principle that people learn by example, but one that is generally ig-

nored in relation to teaching Christianity through the conduct of a rehearsal and the way the director handles situations that arise.

Anyone who has ever conducted classes or workshops for choir directors knows that one of the chief concerns that are voiced is over discipline — meaning control, correction, and punishment. These are particularly difficult questions to answer, because they reflect a misconception of the true meaning and character of Christian discipline, and of its significance in Christian education. Apparently large numbers of choir directors still teach by the stern rule, "Do this and be rewarded; do that and be punished." Others work in pandemonium which results from lack of orderly Christian discipline and knowledge of educational principles.

Christian discipline originates with Christ's call, "Come, follow me," which causes a true disciple to leave behind all habits and customs that are inconsistent with Christ's way. Acceptance of discipleship should mean to us today, as to the early disciples, a continual attempt to remold our personalities into Christ's pattern. Jesus' leadership centered in what he was. He never treated lightly or unkindly the mistakes and faults of others. It was his great love that drew people to him and caused them to learn about the Father through him. Through firm kindness he led people, and in his presence they were at their best.

Christian discipline consists in training in obedience to Christ and in living according to his standards. A Christian leader can find all the rules for good leadership in studying the leadership qualities of Jesus.

Jesus loved all people as creatures of God and for what he knew they could become. He recognized their differences and saw beneath the outward manners to the inmost spiritual and emotional feelings. He could educe the tiniest spark of good in a man and help him to see and develop it. Through his evident love and respect for a man's dignity and essential personality he could help a person to correct a fault without rancor or loss of dignity.

Jesus' simple commands are direct and leave no question as to what he expects of a Christian disciple: "You shall love the Lord your God with all your heart, and with all your soul, and with all your mind . . . and . . . your neighbor as yourself," and "Go therefore and make disciples of all nations, . . . teaching them," clearly point out that we must give ourselves completely over to God before we can teach others. Jesus' love was so all-consuming that he paid the supreme sacrifice that all might be taught the nature of God's love for man. Sacrifice is part of the price we pay as leaders, not only of time and effort but also of self-pride, personal feelings, and the many traits that prevent us from our best leadership.

Jesus told his disciples that when he had gone to his Father the Holy Spirit would be with them to guide them. Effective Christian discipline rests on the guidance by the Holy Spirit and the sincere effort to discover the will of God and to do it. Jesus relied on prayer and Scriptures and taught his disciples to do so. A Christian leader will seek God through the Holy Word and prayer. Regular Bible study and prayer are surely necessary to one who seeks God. One cannot share what he does not have. One cannot lead others into the presence of God through music, unless he has been there himself. One cannot lead others to become Christian disciples unless he practices Christian discipline.

Choir leaders teach discipline most successfully when their disciplinary example and group practices follow the ideals of Jesus. Such a director will:

1. Respect and love the members of his choirs, as God's children, and for the qualities that each possesses, which he hopes to discover and help him develop. This may be an assignment that will cost a great deal of time and thought and ingenuity to work out in a church with large choirs. Finding out what a person is really like is a fascinating pursuit and can be worked at in all kinds of places and times. Short direct conversations with the choir member, his family or friends, conversation between members in the choir room, a card file of interests and observations are a few mechanical get-acquainted devices. The

best way to get to know a person is to observe him in the process of "living" with him. An observing choir director can learn a great deal about a person by his reactions in rehearsals, his facial expressions, what he seems to respond to, his reliability, and his response to recreational experiences. But in all these ways we are apt to judge the man by his outward appearance and reactions. A choir camp is a wonderful place to really get acquainted with children and to relate the disciplines of music to the discipline of Christian living. In a camp there is opportunity and time to carry through to completion the lessons in discipline and the ventures in friendly understanding.

In a series of articles written in the magazine *Diapason* (March, 1955) in tribute to Henry Sloane Coffin, Seth Bingham, who was the organist-director at Madison Avenue Presbyterian Church early in the careers of both men, writes of Dr. Coffin: "Humility is a compelling word which has marked the triumphs of the saints in all ages. I sorely needed humility. When I started trying to *love* my choir into doing things instead of antagonizing them I began to get worth-while results, and discipline became a minor problem. Whatever success I may have achieved in my work at Madison Avenue was due in no small measure to Henry Coffin's kindly encouragement and wise counsel. He had a brotherly gift for guiding you in the way you should go. Let me give you one example:

"The choir's recording secretary was a smart, lively girl with an independent manner. I was strict about unexcused absences. But she would simply tell me, 'I'll be away this week,' without giving any reason. The third time this happened, I quoted our attendance rule, 'No unexcused absences; that goes for you the same as the others.' Out walked Edna. She continued to attend church regularly but cut the choir. Dr. Coffin heard of it. Throwing a friendly arm about my shoulder, he urged me to beg her pardon! I swallowed hard, took a long breath and replied, 'Well, you're the doctor.' After service I sought her out in the congregation. 'Edna, I'm sorry I offended you. I hope you'll pardon me.' She was back on the job at the next rehearsal and became one

of my most faithful members from then on." (Quoted by permission of the author.)

2. The director will relate Christian discipline to the discipline of music in his own experience and in his teaching. Beautiful musical performance is not achieved without regular, consistent practice. Mind, body, and emotions must become thoroughly disciplined for people to become instruments through which music is produced. This kind of discipline is not enough, however, to produce truly beautiful music, for such music is more than a performance. It is also a spiritual expression. This discipline must be freely accepted, or the resulting music will lack the spiritual quality that is present in all truly great music. Going back to a Christian analogy, "Take my yoke upon you, and learn from me; . . . for my yoke is easy, and my burden is light," a musician must freely accept the "yoke" of consistent study and practice and be willing to make costly sacrifices in order to achieve his goal. The "burden" would be heavy indeed were the yoke taken unwillingly.

A person who wishes to achieve a fair degree of musical satisfaction must first learn the meaning of regular and particular practice. In order to do this he has to sacrifice other time-consuming activities which bring pleasure. This is equally true of individuals in a choir group. But here the discipline is a composite of that of the individuals who comprise the group. Each, in his acceptance of the purposes of the group, makes his contribution in proportion to his self-discipline. This is a Christian ideal which reminds us of Paul's First Letter to the Corinthians, in which he speaks of the community of believers in this way, "All the members of the body, though many, are one body," and later, "If one member suffers, all suffer together; if one member is honored, all rejoice together." In these words Paul might well be describing a true choir experience. In a choir each member must accept the discipline imposed by membership — regularity, punctuality, wholehearted participation, the will to achieve, loyalty, and willingness to accept his share of the responsibility. Without acceptance of responsibility, individuals in

a choir cannot realize the necessary sense of achievement. The director who understands the demands and the sacrifices involved in choir membership, because he understands the nature of the competitive demands, will be sympathetic with his singers and will reward their efforts and hard-won results with his sincere praise. He will not take lightly the need for satisfaction, at the same time that he lifts the goals to spur them on.

After an especially glorious, worshipful candlelight vesper service in which some one hundred singers had participated, one particularly sensitive ten-year-old girl looked dreamily at the organist-director and said: "I do hope you'll forgive me. I stopped singing for three notes, because the music was so lovely, I wanted to hear. I hope I didn't spoil anything." The child never doubted that the director knew when she had failed to do her bit. This kind of responsibility for doing one's best for the sake of the composite contribution of the choir is the ingredient that is the result of discipline well learned in a choir.

3. The director will teach the attitude of reverence for God and for all that is holy, by example, as well as by instruction. One of the main functions of the choir is to lead in worship. The seriousness with which the director regards the preparation for the worship service teaches an attitude. It is, however, in conversation and other indirect ways that attitudes are frequently communicated. It is very difficult to undo the damage that may be done by an off-color joke or a parodied song that belittles religion, or by a loss of control in which the name of God is taken in vain. Camps and recreational trips are good places not only to get to know choir members, but choir directors' true personalities and characters also come to light under the same circumstances.

4. He will radiate with the abundant joy and buoyant spirit which give warmth to personality and rightfully characterize Christian discipline in this good-natured, joyous mien which is contagious. This is good for the music as well as the spirit, because the beauty of tone improves tremendously with buoyancy of spirit. The warmth of a Christian personality sheds itself with selfless concern on others. To a man whose contacts with other

people always offer an opportunity to fulfill Christ's command, there is little room in his thoughts for using a choir as a means of glorifying his own reputation or for nursing ill-will against a choir member who acts in a manner that he cannot understand.

5. He will learn to correct the flaws in individuals and the mistakes of the choir, in the spirit of Jesus, leaving no unpleasant memory associations as barriers to further progress. Sarcasm, unkind criticism, making fun of, and showing up another are not, by any means, uncommon with choral directors. Some of the unkind names that directors have called choir members have made indelible impressions on their feelings and in some cases have closed the door to expression of religion through song. Mr. Bingham, in the aforementioned article (which is entitled "Organist's Tribute Paid to a Minister Who Proves an Ideal"), says of Dr. Coffin: "He was by nature thoroughly democratic. He liked people — all sorts of people; they felt this and they warmed to him. In his preaching or conversation he never tried to call attention to himself. (Can we organists claim as much while playing or directing?) He never gave way to sarcasm and violent expressions of prejudice, nor did he 'bawl out' people." What a glorious tribute to a great Christian! Could it be possible that Dr. Coffin was not subject to the same kind of irritating problems that arise in choir groups? I hardly think this possible. Respect for another's feelings, especially in correction, is important. Kindness does not preclude firmness. A well-planned and well-paced rehearsal, a prevailing spirit of good will, do away with the need for stringent corrective measures.

Children's choir directors meet with all the problems that public school directors do, only the volunteer nature of the church organizations increases the number of them. Many circumstances and needs cause the attitudes and behaviors with which the director has to deal in rehearsals. Charles W. Leonard, in *Why Children Misbehave,* p. 29, states that many adults deal only with a child's misbehavior and pay no attention to the reason, and that the fact that they do not accept children as they are, sometimes, causes misbehavior. He also concludes that chil-

dren need to be guided to learn self-restraints and self-discipline. With this we agree, but the Christian goes one step farther and concludes that the only safe discipline is that of Christian discipline, centered in obedience to His command. Unless the choir director points the way beyond himself to Christ, as the final authority, the discipline is centered in himself or in each choir member. The choir director is God's instrument, not " the boss." This makes a choir a democratic organization. It requires more of a director to be a leader than it does to be a " boss," but it is definitely more rewarding.

In summary, the choir director should lovingly consider each individual choir member, and the plan for his development; relate the disciplines of Christianity and of music in his own experience and his teaching; teach reverence by example and instruction; radiate the buoyant joy of Christianity; correct mistakes in the spirit of Christ. He will regard persons in the choir as in the growing stages toward Christian maturity and his own responsibility to be an aid and guide in the growth.

Chapter 16

THE VOICE IN SINGING AND CHORAL SPEECH

The Tone

TONE is the basis of choir work. A choir director must know of what good tone consists, recognize it when he hears it, know how to produce it, and what to do when it is not being produced. It is dangerous to write about tone production, because verbalizing creates the impression that all these things are talked about and taught directly in pedantic manner to the choirs, which is entirely wrong. An example, a suggestion (not always in words) will frequently bring amazing results. Once the principles are understood by the singers, and the results recognized by the director, a sign, a look, a suggestion will get the result. Since this is not a book on vocal technique nor even on choral technique, there can be no lengthy descriptions and explanations of tone production. There are books to which the director of the adult and high school choirs may turn for description and guidance. Some of these are listed in the Bibliography. Children's voices have not been so frequently nor so well described as the others. In general, certain principles of production hold true for all singers.

The Child's Voice

The distribution of the amount of head and body tone changes with age and development. A child's voice is predominantly head tone, light, clear, and lacking in the rich overtones and

undertones that characterize the developed adult voice. It is important that the ideals of correct tone production be planted in singers while they are in the children's choirs and maintained throughout the successive choirs. If a child learns to sing correctly, he will never need to unlearn anything about singing. The voice will develop and become richer with resonance and stronger in a natural way. The same principles of posture, vitalization, breath, focus, facial expression and diction hold for all ages. Each developmental stage has its characteristic tone quality. Voices should never be exploited for the sake of effect. No effect is beautiful that depends on the misuse of the voice. A growing child's voice should be protected, but, on the other hand, it should be used with the full vitality and tone of which he is capable.

Principles of Production

Good tone production depends on the proper application of principles which singers sometimes study for years to comprehend fully and apply, but which can be sufficiently learned and applied by children and adults in choirs, to produce beautiful singing tone. The following descriptions are for the choir director, not to be passed on in this form to choir singers.

Posture. This is important because the body is the musical instrument that produces the tone. The back must be straight, head high, chin in, shoulders spread, chest high (off the rib cage). Stretching up through the middle adjusts the chest. The chest should stay up when breathing to sing.

Energy. It takes energy to produce a tone. The body must be vitalized, not tense, not limp. Much off-key, colorless, weak singing results from limpness. Raspy, breathy, nasal, and pushed tones result from misapplied energy, overtension. Vitalization is greatly affected by the emotions. A pleasant, carefree, but thoughtful vocalization period will produce it. Two or three physical exercises before singing will help — stand on tiptoe and push up an imaginary ceiling, or bend at the waist (but not the knees) and touch the toes.

Breathing. Standing as described above, under "Posture," breathe through the nostrils, expand around the rib cage, and allow the breath to go as deep as it will, also expanding the abdomen. Keep the chest up. Now inhale and exhale that way several times. In singing, the inhaling is quick and the exhaling very slow and controlled because the tone is on the exhaled breath. Think of the process as a series of quick, automatic vitalizations to sing, followed by relaxation. The breath should never be audible and never will be, so long as this breathing formula is followed.

Tone. The body supplies the energy, the emotions vitalize it, and the breath flows through the body, along the spinal column, resounding in the resonance chambers.

Focus. The tone is focused in a spot at the top of the spine, above the roof of the mouth. Tone is its loveliest when the singer does not push to send the tone out, but allows it to resound freely in the body and come out naturally. The vowel that helps most to find the focal point is $\overline{oo}$. Children should use $\overline{oo}$ frequently to refocus the voice. The breath must flow freely and continuously. Held breath causes overtensions. After $\overline{oo}$ the other vowel sounds should be practiced. To go from oo to ah without loss of high focus is an important lesson to learn. The different consonant sounds are then placed in front of the vowels. The m and n combined with $\overline{ee}$ and $\overline{a}$ help increase head resonance. Consonant sounds are the servants of resonance and diction. It is best to work on them in connection with specific places in songs.

Facial Expression. Facial expression affects the tone of a singer. The jaw must not be tense, but should feel as if it were hung from the ears. The nostrils should be slightly inflated, the cheek muscles held high, the upper lip free from the teeth, and the mouth open. This is simply a description of how one looks when a pleasant thought passes through the mind (except for the open mouth). It cannot be stressed enough that these are not directions to be given to choir singers, but rather a description of the feeling and look of tone production by which the choir

director identifies the singers' results. *Sensitivity* to the blending of the voices in the group can be acquired and will prevent individual voices from standing out because of unpleasant tone. Listen with keenly sensitive ears to your choirs, and train them to listen to each other. Don't rehearse continually with the piano, and never with loud accompaniment with children.

A large share of the director's responsibility in a performance of children is for the constant correct production of tone. The children of his choir are singing in other situations more frequently than they are with him, and therefore may need on-the-spot reminders of his ideal of production.

The Director Suggests Tone. The director gains his results readily and effectively through constant alertness to tone quality. In rehearsal he works until it is established and then tries to maintain it. In performance he expects it and looks as if he does. He breathes with his singers, he stands with good posture, he has the facial expression that his singers should have, and with a few simple movements of his hands, he reminds the singers to elongate or round the tone, to stretch the body for fuller tone, to focus higher. But usually they need no signs other than a sincere look of enjoyment and trust on the face of the director.

The Organist-Director. The organist-director who has his choir in front of him can manage to convey suggestions through facial expression and an occasional gesture, but the choirs behind him are on their own in performance for everything except occasional cues from the organist. There are differing opinions about the desirability of the long-range direction. In so far as it encourages group feeling and reliance, without sacrifice to beauty, it is good. In any event the director should work out his effects in rehearsal and help the singers to establish them securely. On the other hand, volunteer choir singers are not mature musicians and rarely give their best performance without close-range direction. A Toscanini-trained orchestra of first-rate musicians has developed, through long hours of rigid, disciplined rehearsal and study, the group feeling to join their individual spiritual and musical resources into a perfection of

oneness that can produce performance without visible direction. A group of singers that rehearses together for long hours daily can achieve the same unity. A group of volunteer church singers rehearsing together, one or even three hours a week, can scarcely be expected to arrive at the ability to achieve their best performance without the aid of a director who has achieved greater musical maturity than the singers and can guide the democratic process but not interfere with it.

The organist-director of many choirs, some of which must perform remote from his direction, needs an assistant who attends his rehearsals and is thoroughly acquainted with his principles of tone production and his interpretations. The assistant could well be a pianist, who accompanies in rehearsals, and is serving a sort of apprenticeship, to learn more about music and singing, or a member of the adult choir who is skilled in dealing with children.

Choral Speech

Closely related to the art of choral singing is that of choral speech. Although it is an ancient art which traces its lineage of descent from the Greek chorus, and has been preserved in its freest and least pure form in the worship services of the Christian church, in the responsive readings and prayer recitations, it is being received with fresh enthusiasm today, as if it were a new art.

Churches are rediscovering the beauty and value which choral reading can contribute to worship. Speech choirs are being added to Christian education programs, and singing choirs are including choral readings in their musical repertoires. The benefits derived by the cultivation of choral speech by a singing choir work in two directions. Where choral reading is thoroughly studied and prepared, the beauty of the resulting speech rests upon, among other things, the clarity of diction and purity of tone. The readers become aware of the meanings of words and their dependence on tone and diction for beautiful expression. This can only strengthen the use of words with meaningful ex-

pression in song. On the other hand, the cultivated tonal production and rhythmic expression of the singing choir lends beauty to choral speech.

The values of choral reading as an educational medium are great enough to cause Christian educators to include it in curriculum materials. Appreciation of Scripture passages and of religious poetry is greatly enhanced through study for choral reading. Group memorization is enjoyable and easy when concentrating on the meaning and interpretation of the passage rather than upon the laborious process of conscious memorization. Speakers feel secure in the company of others who give expression to the reading, and the individuals are carried along with the group.

There is danger that the great values of choral speech will lure the uninitiated into using it before adequate preparation has been made. The teacher of choral reading should endeavor to learn all he can about it before presenting it to a choir. Fortunately, a person who knows how to produce a good speaking tone, who understands and loves poetry, and is willing to do some reading on the subject, can make a start in leading choral speech. Directors of singing choirs have good equipment for the start, but they must remember that in choral reading the interpretation comes before the rhythm and meter, in importance. Marjorie Gullan's *The Speech Choir* is an excellent introduction to the art of choral speech. Winifred Ward's *Playmaking with Children* has a very helpful chapter (Ch. 11) on the development of good speech for choral speaking. *Choral Reading for Worship and Inspiration,* edited by Helen A. Brown and Harry J. Heltman, contains choral arrangements of Bible passages and religious poetry as well as suggestions to the director on choral technique. Other books of choral readings by Helen A. Brown and Harry J. Heltman, including *Choral Readings from the Bible* and *Choral Readings for Fun and Recreation,* also give suggestions on how to use this kind of material.

The material to be used for choral interpretation should be selected for its real literary worth and for its appeal to the en-

thusiasm of the children. The words, imagery, rhythm, phrasing, and arrangement of line, all contribute to the expression of the poem. The passage to be learned should have lasting value in the literary repertoire of the speakers. It should be a suitable expression of the group rather than of an individual.

The same fundamentals required for tone production in song are necessary for good speech. Good posture, correct breathing, freedom from restraint, and clear diction are essentials. As has been stated earlier in this chapter it is the consonants that give the clarity to diction. Games may be made of consonant drills. The old tongue twisters like "Peter Piper picked a peck of pickled peppers" and "She sells sea shells by the seashore" are helpful in developing diction. A trilled r makes the tongue flexible. M and n help focus tone high. The plosives p, b, t, d, k, g, bring the flow of breath through to produce vital tone. Reading a passage through with each consonant separated slightly from the vowels makes readers conscious of their production. For example,

P-ēē-t-er P-i-p-er p-i-ck-d a p-e-ck o-v p-i-ck-l-d p-e-pp-er-s

Now connect the consonants and vowels and the words of the phrase with a continuous flow of breath, but keep distinct consonant sounds. Smooth flowing, but clearly enunciated phrases should result.

In presenting a passage to the choir for speakers to learn, the director allows the group to study silently, then discuss the interpretation. Thus the teacher does not get a "parrotlike" response from his group. Simplicity, sincerity, and naturalness are to be desired. Beauty of tone is desired above volume.

Good examples of combinations of speech with choral music may be found in the series of junior anthem books published by The Westminster Press, Books 1, 2, and 3.

The following arrangement for speech and singing choirs was used as part of a Christmas candlelight service in the First Presbyterian Church of Youngstown, Ohio. The organ background indicated was an improvisation in E flat. In lieu of the improvisation, the music in *Anthems for the Junior Choir,* Book 2, p. 29,

may be played in free style and very softly, coming to a sustained E flat chord when the speakers say "lying in a manger." The anthem to be sung is the one on p. 29 of Book 2. The singing choir proceeds from the E flat chord without a break. The speakers were senior high school students. The singers were the junior and junior high school choirs.

THE CHRISTMAS STORY

Luke 2:1–20

SOLO VOICE 1:

In those days a decree went out from Caesar Augustus that all the world should be enrolled. This was the first enrollment, when Quirinius was governor of Syria. And all went to be enrolled, each to his own city. And Joseph also went up from Galilee, from the city of Nazareth, to Judea, to the city of David, which is called Bethlehem, because he was of the house and lineage of David, to be enrolled with Mary, his betrothed, who was with child. And while they were there, the time came for her to be delivered. And she gave birth to her first-born son and wrapped him in swaddling cloths, and laid him in a manger, because there was no place for them in the inn.

SPEECH CHOIR (*organ background in key of E flat through this next*):

And in that region there were shepherds out in the field, keeping watch over their flock by night. And an angel of the Lord appeared to them, and the glory of the Lord shone around them, and they were filled with fear. And the angel said to them,

SOLO VOICE 2:

"Be not afraid; for behold, I bring you good news of a great joy which will come to all the people; for to you is born this day in the city of David a Savior, who is Christ the Lord. And this will be a sign for you: you will find a babe wrapped in swaddling cloths and lying in a manger."

SINGING CHOIR (*from Anthem Book 2*):

And suddenly there was with the angel a multitude of the heavenly host praising God and saying,

"Glory to God in the highest,
and on earth peace among men with whom he is pleased!"

(*End organ.*)

Solo Voice 3:
When the angels went away from them into heaven, the shepherds said to one another,
Speech Choir:
"Let us go over to Bethlehem and see this thing that has happened, which the Lord has made known to us."
Solo Voice 3:
And they went with haste, and found Mary and Joseph, and the babe lying in a manger.
Speech Choir:
And when they saw it they made known the saying which had been told them concerning this child; and all who heard it wondered at what the shepherds told them.
Solo Voice 4:
But Mary kept all these things, pondering them in her heart.
Speech Choir:
And the shepherds returned, glorifying and praising God for all they had heard and seen, as it had been told them.

"Glory to God in the highest,
and on earth peace among men with whom he is pleased!"

Chapter 17

CHOIR ORGANIZATION AND REHEARSAL

THE ORGANIZATION of the choir program of the church will necessarily be affected by the potential leadership, the number of people available in the age levels of the prospective choirs, and the official attitude toward the formation of choirs.

Where choirs are seriously considered as a means for furthering the growth toward Christian maturity, a church will need to have more than one choir in order to serve the different age levels. The multiple choir system is the result.

A multiple choir system is a plan for the organization of several choirs in one church and for the progression of choir members from one choir to the next, with their growth. The aim is to furnish choir opportunities for all ages and groups within the church, and according to congenial age groupings.

The number of choirs in the system and the plan of classification differ according to the size of the church and age groups. In determining the groupings it is wise to consider that too wide a span of ages is not good in one choir because of lack of congeniality of interest and skill development. On the other hand, some difference of ages is good (if not too great). The older persons in the group are a spur to the younger ones, and the younger ones add enthusiasm and prevent the group from becoming too intimate and exclusive.

The singing choirs should serve all people from third grade through adults. Children below third grade may have a choir of

their own, the purpose of which is different from the others. The divisions into choirs will differ in different churches, and at times will vary within the church.

The following choir classifications are the ones most commonly used. Many churches give choirs names that do not refer to age. The grade names are used here for clarity.

The Departmental Plan:

Choir One — Grades 4, 5, and 6 (Junior)
Choir Two — Grades 7, 8, and 9 (Junior High)
Choir Three — Grades 10, 11, and 12 (Senior High)
Choir Four — All above high school (Adult)

This plan permits a close relationship between choirs and the church school and youth fellowship. This has the advantage of facilitating the Sunday program and the making of contacts through the school organization.

The Voice Classification Plan:

Choir One — Grades 4–8, unchanged voices
Choir Two — Grades 9–12, youth choir, mixed voices
Choir Three — adult, mixed voices

This plan clearly classifies the choir division and facilitates repertoire selection. It is especially adapted to smaller churches, where close gradation makes choirs too small.

The Modified Voice Classification Plan:

Choir One — Grades 3–6, unchanged voices
Choir Two — Grades 7–8, unchanged voices
Choir Three — Grades 9–12, mixed voices
Choir Four — Adults (all above high school)

A post-high choir may be added in any church that has enough young people to warrant it. The modified plan is the most fluid of the classification plans and the most easily adapted. Its advantage over plan II is that the girls of the seventh and eighth grades are given an opportunity to move along at their own pace, which is more rapid than that of the juniors, because of greater

experience. At the same time they may be used in performance, along with the juniors, to add body to tone and part-song facility. In addition, they may learn an independent repertoire, for they learn easily. At times they may be used along with the youth choir. They are a versatile group with large capacity, which was developed during the junior choir.

The multiple choir system is properly thought of as a unified organization of several units, meeting to rehearse separately, but fulfilling the same functions and existing for the same purposes. Lines of demarcation cannot be set fast. Some of the organization's program and repertoire includes all, some parts are for specific units.

Choir mothers are needed for all choirs. Those who serve in the children's and youth's choirs have responsibilities that they should be invited to assume for a definite term with defined duties. In some churches, choir mothers are assigned by the Women's Association, and their names appear in the Association Yearbook.

The number of mothers needed to help any one choir is determined by the number of choir members and the nature of assignments. The duties include:

1. Responsibility for robes: condition; assignment.
2. Assisting with robing children for services.
3. Responsibility for maintaining choir morale when the director is fulfilling duties outside the choir room.
4. Marshaling the choir to and from the choir room on festival occasions.
5. Lighting candles for candlelight processions.
6. Transporting singers to other churches and places for choir festivals and rallies.
7. Planning and giving choir parties.

If there are fifty children in a choir, at least six mothers are needed. In a youth choir of the same number, four mothers will be enough. One mother should be appointed chairman and be the one who keeps in contact with the director for schedule of

events. She, in turn, notifies the other mothers and provides substitutes when necessary. In some churches the chairman is responsible for working out car pools.

Activity Chart

The choir program should be planned in accord with the total church program and in consultation with the minister and the committee. The year's plan should be charted by months and weeks and the predetermined events sketched in at one time. In most churches there are certain traditional seasonal events that are church-wide and include the choirs. The large " All Choir " chart will help to distribute the singing responsibilities between the choirs according to their capacities for meeting the demands. In addition there will be some special demands for family events, extra services, and series of vesper services, such as oratorios and cantatas. The parts in these to be sung by the different choirs will be determined and they will then be written in on the chart. Some churches plan to have the children and youth choirs each sing once a month in morning worship services. These services are then distributed between the choirs, keeping their other heavy responsibilities in mind. After the main responsibilities have been scheduled, service projects, choir festivals, rallies, parties, and any secular musical activities may be added to the chart. A wise director schedules a full program of choir activities so that all his singers will respect the significance of the choir and their need to work for it. On the other hand the director must know when " enough is enough," and not attempt the impossible, in order to avoid work being poorly done and singers losing their sense of satisfaction in the music.

Singers' Records

Each choir member is important in himself, as well as part of the group. His individual capacities and growth are matters of record for the choir director. Some choir directors have a registration card for the choir children, signed by parents and children. The card contains a statement of acceptance of the re-

sponsibilities of a choir member and lists them. These cards are either mailed home with a letter explaining the choir purposes and obligations, or, better still, they are signed at a meeting of parents and choir mothers where the purposes and year's program are discussed. Adult choir registration cards are also excellent for emphasing choir responsibility.

If the choir director auditions his singers, his first observations are written on the back of the card. Every sign of musical or personal growth is recorded thereafter. (We have not found it advisable to have audition tryouts for children's choirs for several reasons: among them, that children rarely ever can respond in an audition without embarrassment or fright, which render the audition valueless.) We do not wish our first contact with a child to be embarrassing or burdened with a barrier. We have found that we can take all who wish to sing, with practically no harm to the organization, and if they do not learn to be good contributing members, they either do not sing enough to harm it, or else join another organization. After the singer has entered the choir, opportunities may be created when, under relaxed circumstances, individuals may be heard alone or in small groups. Adults and youths should be auditioned and the person placed in the section that the choir director thinks best.

The Audition

The voice tryout is a private interview in which the director decides, to the best of his ability, the part which the singer will sing in the choir. The placement is difficult to determine in one audition, and the director will hear the individuals (especially high school youths) at least twice a year in addition to observing them in rehearsals.

The placement, by parts, depends on quality as well as range and the ease with which one sings continually in a given range. The director puts the singer at ease with conversation, which helps the two to become better acquainted. A good approach is to have the singer select a familiar hymn and sing it. Then starting in a middle range, he sings a series of scales, first progress-

ing downward (starting with the speaking level). After finding the low extreme, the scales are sung upward from the speaking level to determine the high extreme. Sequences of tonic chord arpeggios, sung lightly and rapidly, will help suggest the potential extension of the high range. A legato tonic chord, progressing downward and lingering on the bottom tone, brings to light the possible depth of the voice.

It is the timbre and texture of tone as well as the flexibility and ease in given ranges that determine the part to which the singer is assigned. Herbert Witherspoon identifies voices by what he calls the "lift of the breath" (*Thirty-six Lessons in Singing*), which he explains as the point at which the voice passes from the speaking range. The breath support increases to preserve correct vocal position, the vocal organs exaggerate their movements for higher pitches and at one particular note in the scale "the sound seems to gain in facial resonance, and the vowel modifies slightly." The pitch at which the lift occurs is generally: sopranos and tenors—C sharp or D; baritone and mezzo-sopranos—B; high basses and contraltos—A; low basses and contraltos—G. Of course, the men's voices are an octave lower, in pitch, than the ladies'.

Attendance Records

Attendance records are important because they are symbols of two very important responsibilities, punctuality and regularity of attendance. The attendance book should be kept meticulously by the director with the names of the singers, their full addresses, and telephone numbers. One of the important duties of the choir director is to keep in touch with all singers and to check on absentees, call on the sick, and otherwise show his interest in their welfare.

Awards

After the discourse on Christian discipline, it is undoubtedly redundant to mention the matter of choir awards, merit and demerit systems, and small stipends for volunteer choir singers. Since these subjects are frequently the subject of inquiries, they are mentioned here. Many of us have gone through stages in

which we have relied upon such devices. We now regard the choir system as an integral part of the Christian music education program of the church. It is no longer consistent with the principles of secular education or of Christian education to offer material rewards as goals or for the purpose of stimulating choir membership or interest. A vitally stimulating and strongly active choir program is tremendously more attractive and effective and its results more lasting than awards. It is inconsistent with the real purposes of choirs to hold out as a purpose the gain of something material or even of a symbol of personal recognition. This is not saying that spontaneous recognition and praise that is deserved should not come freely from the director and from pleased and uplifted congregations. Even a choir camp is offered as an extension of the choir program, rather than a reward to the faithful, although faithfulness is a requirement of choir membership. An unhealthy attitude arises from striving for a reward. Recreational and fellowship events are planned for the value that comes to the group spirit, not as a goal to work for. The rewards of good choir membership are many and lasting and come as a by-product to those who strive to fulfill the real purposes of choir membership. Not the least of these rewards is the possession of a repertoire and appreciation of beautiful music to enrich the devotional life of the singer.

The Choir Rehearsal

The choir rehearsal is the workshop activity of the choir. All that a choir is and hopes to become is governed and conditioned by what goes on in the rehearsal. It is in the rehearsal period that the director puts into practice all the principles of education and psychology, music education and Christian discipline of which we speak in other chapters. There are certain practical considerations of the rehearsal, such as the number and length of rehearsals and the plan.

Rehearsal Time. The number and time of rehearsals are determined by the distance that the majority of singers live from the church and the time the director has to devote to them. Chil-

dren's choir rehearsals are frequently on Saturday mornings, and this poses the great problem of competitive groups—dancing, music lessons, swimming, and countless others. In one church a staggered plan was worked out to accommodate the groups, when they could come. This was hard on the director, but resulted in an unusually well trained choir. Hour-long rehearsals were on Wednesday afternoon and Saturday morning, and a one-half hour rehearsal on Sunday morning. Children could join either the Wednesday or Saturday choir and all attended the Sunday morning. All rehearsal absences had to be made up. The result was that fifty per cent of the choir came voluntarily and regularly to all the rehearsals. The remainder made up all absences. Tone improved rapidly and a large memorized repertoire resulted.

During the war, Sunday morning was the only rehearsal time that was feasible. The family car could come to the church just once during the week and had to take care of church, church school, and choir. Some churches still find that Sunday morning is the only satisfactory time for rehearsals.

A large number of youth choirs meet on Sunday evening before or after youth group meetings. Again, it is a case of working it out to get the singers when they can come.

Adult choirs rehearse in proportion to the program they have. Undoubtedly one practice a week is the average. Many, however, rehearse two hours on a weeknight and one hour on Sunday morning before church.

Children's choirs should not rehearse longer than one hour as a usual thing. There are exceptions when preparation is being made for special events. Young people are hard to get together for more than an hour.

The younger children's choir should meet for three quarters of an hour, or an hour, for rhythmic development through toy orchestra, rhythmic play and interpretation, dramatization, and tone work (pitch discrimination and production). It is well to schedule this rehearsal, if possible, for the same time that their older brothers and sisters are rehearsing.

Rehearsal Plan. The amount that is accomplished in rehearsal depends to a great extent on the plans and efficiency of the director. His knowledge of psychology and education are fully as important as his knowledge of music when it comes to rehearsal time. His plan consists of an over-all, long-range yearly or semiyearly schedule, and a specific plan for each week. Keeping in mind the ways people learn and the approaches that are most successful with the age with which he is working (refer to *The Children We Teach,* by Elizabeth Whitehouse), he plans to include in each rehearsal the singing of well-learned music for the joy of the singing, vocalization for tonal warming up, some sort of presentation of a new song, with discussion about words, thorough, particular practice on a part of a song that is being learned, work on diction through consonants, diphthongs, and vowels; in children's rehearsals including the singing of familiar rounds to develop independence in part singing, some ear training, some individual or small group singing, polishing of a song, and memorization.

The distribution of the component parts of a rehearsal and the length of time devoted to each depends on the needs of the group and the prevailing spirit at the time. The good director is sensitive to the singers and knows when a change is needed, how long to work with hard concentration, when to introduce an element of fun, when a prayer is needed and appropriate — in fact, knows the singers!

A tape recorder and a record player are two pieces of equipment that are helpful, provided they are used sparingly. Both are time-consuming devices. Recorded church services in which the choir has participated may be listened to before or after a rehearsal and are very interesting and educational to the singers. Once in a while (rarely), it is well to record in a rehearsal, play it back, do it again and let the singers hear differences in tone and interpretation. Tone improves tremendously when singers can hear themselves. The record player supplies artistic examples for the singers, and spurs them on to better singing.

In a one-hour rehearsal of children's choirs there is little time for

emphasis upon teaching the children to read music. In many and devious ways, suggestions and helps to reading are offered. Since many choir children study instrumental music and learn to read in that way, reading in the choir seems to be no problem. Each child holds a copy of the music when the song is discussed and studied. The object of the study is to arrive quickly at a knowledge of the song and to put the book aside, because music is not what is seen on paper but what can be heard. Sensitivity to tone and to each other is never so evident as when singers have memorized the song. Memorization is essential to good choir singing. " Too often, both adults and children are led to believe that they can learn about music through reading, whereas the procedure is exactly the reverse: one must learn about reading through music. If you want to enjoy reading music, let your learning be the consequence of a great deal of experience in music." (From *Children and Music* by Beatrice Landeck, p. 244. Copyright Beatrice Landeck; published by William Sloane Associates, 1952. Used by permission.)

Chapter 18

CHOIR REPERTOIRE

THE MULTIPLE choirs may be regarded in two ways. Like a many-headed hydra, they are separate choirs, but are really all one big choir working for the same purpose, for the same church, and at times singing the same repertoire. Repertoire must be selected to meet all needs.

Part and Unison Singing

Whether or not to sing part songs in the children's choir is a matter to be decided according to the circumstances. Beautiful tone and beautiful music are of prime importance. If the children can sing in parts without sacrificing beauty of tone, and without spending an unwarranted amount of rehearsal time, part music can add a great deal of interest. The choice of repertoire also affects the decision. Part singing may be easily achieved by the use of certain devices and it provides a real sense of satisfaction from accomplishment. Certainly no child in a children's choir should be assigned to sing alto continually, and be asked to remain silent at all times when there is no alto part. Many good children's anthems are written with two parts, neither of which is low. The children may sing the parts interchangeably. Descants furnish a delightfully satisfying part-song effect and they are easy to sing independently. Anthems that combine unison and two-part, with thirds and sixths predominant, are easy to learn. Canons and rounds of all kinds furnish good two- and three-part material for children. Conversational type anthems, culminating in two parts sung simultaneously, are excellent.

Clarence Dickinson's arrangement of a sacred folk song transcribed by Rüdinger, "Who Knocks So Loud" (The H. W. Gray Co., Inc.), is so written and may be a conversation between boys and girls.

The seventh- and eighth-grade girls bolster the part singing and can do some beautiful two-part work on their own. Some churches are fortunate enough to have boys of these ages to sing an alto part and produce three-part music — soprano, soprano, alto. The youth choir definitely needs to do part work because of the changed voices of the boys and the lowered voices of some of the girls. A predominance of three-part work is done in churches with this group: soprano, alto, baritone. A real tenor is scarce in a high school group. Alto-tenor is not so scarce and a choir director who can search out or arrange four-part music within suitable range for the alto-tenor voice will be rewarded for his effort. This voice is so fleeting in its duration that it is here today and by next week may have moved down into a baritone. S.A.B. music is useful in adult choirs also. Many volunteer adult organizations are without any real tenor and would do better not to attempt four-part music. A variety of part-song effects can be achieved when choirs are combined. A great deal of this music is simple and all the more delightful for it. Sowerby's "The Snow Lay on the Ground" in an S.A.B. arrangement is a very attractive Christmas anthem suitable for a combination of the children's and youth choirs. It is in several stanzas, and variety is achieved by addition of a descant. Further variety may be achieved by giving the adult choir one of the stanzas. This anthem is an excellent example of a harmonized arrangement that is easily sung. The soprano and alto parts progress in easy intervals — thirds, sixth, and unisons are frequent. The baritone is very singable, in root position of chords I — V — IV and in ground bass.

Unison music is beautiful, but harmony adds richness and color. Unison is all the more lovely for the contrast of part music.

Selection of Repertoire

The selection of the repertoire is a part of the director's responsibility which requires considerable study, experience, taste, and judgment. Since the standards for good taste are discussed in Chapter 12 they are omitted here. The following details should be considered in selecting the choral repertory for the year:

1. The number of general praise anthems to meet the performance needs. Some repetition is good, but not too much.

2. Special seasonal anthems are necessary and delightful additions but should be kept in proportion to the total repertoire. Repetition of seasonal anthems is more acceptable than an equal amount of regular service anthems.

3. There should be a good distribution of styles, periods and composers, and new and familiar anthems. The size of the music budget affects this to some extent.

4. The theological concepts and word phraseology, as well as the music, should be appropriate to the worship service of the church, the occasion, and the age of the singers.

5. Hymns should have an important place in the repertoire.

6. The number of new anthems that can be well learned by any choir in a given time will definitely affect the selection. In a choir camp where juniors rehearsed two times a day for six days, a repertoire of fifteen new anthems was completely memorized in addition to hymns, folk songs, and bell-ringing tunes. This was in addition to a full program of recreational, devotional, and creative activities.

This treatise on choirs is not thought to be exhaustive. It is intended to help the choir director to organize his own ideas and ideals and to stimulate his creativity in his profession. Even disagreement will be stimulating and helpful, provided it leads the director into defining his own position. The director who has had

less preparation and experience may be helped to see his position in its relationship to the church and as a Christian educator.

A List of Anthems for Children's, Youth, and Adult Choirs

Choir Combinations

"Eternal Father," Gustav Holst. Choirs, organ, bells (ad lib.). G. Schirmer, Inc., 8510. Unison children and young people; four-part adults; soprano soloist; junior high girls on three-part alleluias.

"Thou, Lord, Art Our Shepherd," Christian Gregor. Early American Moravian Church Music, edited and arranged by Clarence Dickinson. The H. W. Gray Co., Inc. Two-part young people, four-part adults.

"O the Blessedness Is Great," Johann Bechler. Early American Moravian Church Music. Unison or two-part children, four-part adults.

"Blessed Jesus," F. Melius Christiansen. Augsburg Publishing House. Four-part adults antiphonally with children.

"O Saviour Sweet," Bach-Dickinson, The H. W. Gray Co., Inc. Unison children, four-part adults (general and Lent).

"Psalm 150," W. Lawrence Curry. The H. W. Gray Co., Inc., 2129. Unison children, four-part adults (festival and general).

"Light of Light," Bach-Norman. Neil A. Kjos Music Co., 5100. Two-part children and junior high girls, four-part adults.

"Surely the Lord Is in This Place," Coke-Jephcott. The H. W. Gray Co., Inc., CMR 1974. Antiphonal effects. Unison children and young people, chanting; four-part adults (general and festival).

"As It Fell Upon a Night," English folk song arranged by Katherine K. Davis. Galaxy Music Corp., 1291. Unison children, four-part adults. Last stanza a canon, adapts well to bells (Christmas).

"Above the Clear Blue Sky," Don Malin. C. C. Birchard & Company, 2092. Children and youth, S.A.B. and unison children and young people. (Christmas).

"Christ, the Lord, Is Born," Roberta Bitgood. Galaxy Music Corp., 1945. Unison children, four-part adults (start children on soprano on page 4) (Christmas).

"The Winter Passes Over," Richard Purvis. Leeds Music Corp., L 109. Unison children, S.S.A. junior high girls, four-part adults (Lent).

Unison Anthems

"Jubilato Deo," Richard Purvis. Leeds Music Corp., L 134. All ages enjoy. Low voices drop out in the two high phrases (general and thanksgiving).

"My Shepherd Will My Need Supply," traditional hymn tune from Southern U.S.A., arranged by Thomson. Use in unison although written in four parts. One stanza may be used in harmony with adult choir. The H. W. Gray Co., Inc., CMR 2046.

"Masters in This Hall," Gustav Holst. G. Schirmer, Inc., 8469. All choirs or any one in unison (Christmas).

"Christmas Song," Gustav Holst. G. Schirmer Music Company. Children (Christmas).

"Lightly, Lightly Bells Are Pealing," Moravian. Arranged by Charlotte Garden. The H. W. Gray Co., Inc. (Christmas).

"On Christmas Night," R. Vaughan Williams. Galaxy Music Corp.

"A Bright Star Shining," Matthews. The H. W. Gray Co., Inc., 404. Use in unison although written in four parts.

Two-Part

"Brother James's Air" (23d Psalm), Bain-Jacob. Unison with descant (may also be procured in four parts). Oxford University Press, New York.

"Long Hast Thou Stood, O Church of God," Ludvig Lindeman, arranged by Katherine K. Davis. Unison with descant (also obtainable in four-part arrangement). E. C. Schirmer Music Company.

"Let All Things Now Living," Welsh melody arranged by Katherine K. Davis. E. C. Schirmer Music Company. Also obtainable in four parts (general and thanksgiving).

"Joyful, Joyful We Adore Thee," Beethoven-Lutkin. H. T. FitzSimons Co., Chicago. Junior high girls.

"God Is My Shepherd," Dvořák. The H. W. Gray Co., Inc., 1886. Junior high girls or advanced juniors.

"O Nightingale, Awake," Swiss Christmas carol, arranged by Dickinson. The H. W. Gray Co., Inc., 213. Junior high girls.

Soprano, Alto, Baritone

"To the Blessed Trinity," Robert Saunders. C. C. Birchard & Company.

"Praise the Lord, Ye Heavens Adore Him," Welsh tune arranged by Pritchard. With descant. C. C. Birchard & Company (general and thanksgiving).

"My Soul, Awake and Render," Bach. E. C. Schirmer Music Company, 493.

"Jesu, Joy of Man's Desiring," Bach. E. C. Schirmer Music Company, 2258.

"God Be with Thee!" Grazioli. E. C. Schirmer Music Company, 1704.

"Mighty Spirit, All Transcending" (Ave Verum), Mozart. E. C. Schirmer Music Company, 2244.

"Lo, a Voice to Heaven Sounding," Bortniansky. E. C. Schirmer Music Company, 1758.

"Praise to the Lord," Bach. E. C. Schirmer Music Company, 2263.

"Prayer of Thanksgiving," Netherlands Tune. E. C. Schirmer Music Company, 1737. With descant (general and thanksgiving).

"To Thee, O Lord, Do I Lift Up My Soul," Kalinikoff. J. Fischer & Bro., 7156.

"The Snow Lay on the Ground," Sowerby. The H. W. Gray Co., Inc., 2313. With descant (Christmas).

"Who Knocks So Loud," folk song from the Tyrol, arranged by Clarence Dickinson. The H. W. Gray Co., Inc., 213 (Christmas).

"Pat-a-Pan," Burgundian Christmas carol. E. C. Schirmer Music Company, 2297.

"While by Our Sleeping Flock We Lay," seventeenth century German carol. E. C. Schirmer Music Company, 2235.

Soprano, Alto, Tenor, Bass (Not Difficult)

"Lord of Hosts," Wennerberg. Neil A. Kjos Music Co., 5081. Youth or adult choir.

"My Shepherd Will My Need Supply," Thomson. The H. W. Gray Co., Inc.

"Treasures in Heaven," Clokey. C. C. Birchard & Company (general and Lent).

"I Will Lift Up Mine Eyes," Sowerby. Boston Music Company.

"We Have No Other Help but Thee," Archangelsky. Witmark and Sons.

"Blessed Art Thou, O Lord God," Purvis. The H. W. Gray Co., Inc.

"The Angels Sang a Gloria," W. Lawrence Curry. The H. W. Gray

Co., Inc., 1602. Unison children, four-part adults (Christmas).

"Ding, Dong Merrily on High," French carol, Geer. E. C. Schirmer Music Company, 1598. Also S.S.A. and can be unison (Christmas).

"See Jesus the Saviour," Appalachian folk tune, J. J. Niles. G. Schirmer, Inc., A-303 (Christmas).

"A Bright Star Shining," Matthews. The H. W. Gray Co., Inc., 404 (Christmas).

"None Other Lamb," Garth Edmundson. J. Fischer & Bro. (Lent).

"Chorales from the *St. Matthew Passion,*" Bach. G. Schirmer, Inc.

"O Holy Jesu," Lvoff. G. Schirmer, Inc. (Communion and Lent).

"Easter Chorales," Bach. J. Fischer & Bro.

Anthem Collections

Anthems for the Junior Choir, W. Lawrence Curry, editor. The Westminster Press. Books 1, 2, and 3.

Junior Choir Anthem Book, John Holler. The H. W. Gray Co., Inc. Book II (unison), Book I (two-part).

We Praise Thee, A Junior Choir Book for the Church Year, by Healey Willan. Concordia Publishing House.

Anthems for the Youth Choir, Book I, W. Lawrence Curry, editor. The Westminster Press. S.A.B.

Junior Choir Anthem Book III, John Holler. The H. W. Gray Co., Inc. S.A.B.

Anthems for the Mixed Choir, W. Lawrence Curry, editor. The Westminster Press.

Dr. Curry, Music Editor for the Board of Christian Education of the Presbyterian Church in the U.S.A., Witherspoon Building, Philadelphia 7, Pennsylvania, has compiled a comprehensive list of anthems for general and special uses and for choirs of all kinds, entitled *Choral Repertoire and Service Material.*

Collections of Responses and Descants

Service Music for the Adult Choir, Introits, Responses, Amens, edited by W. Lawrence Curry. The Westminster Press.

Familiar Hymns with Descants, by Donald D. Kettring. The Westminster Press.

CONCLUSION

MUSIC education should take place in every phase and activity of the life and program of the church. All who are concerned with church worship services, Sunday church school, organization of the church, and with choirs should know the purposes of music in the church program and should try to discover the ways to implement the total program with significant experiences with music.

Music can make so vital a contribution to religion that all individuals of a church congregation should be given the opportunity to learn how to participate well. The music of all churches, regardless of size, should lift the aesthetic taste of the people to a level worthy of religious expression. The church school and the choirs help to inculcate in children and youth the relationship of music to religion and life, and to develop their abilities to use it.

Unity of purpose and plan are needed for the most effective use of music in the church. A committee representing the organizations of the church should study the existing use of music and make a long-range plan to develop the program.

Skills should be developed in choirs of disciplined singers who dedicate their talents and time to beautifying the worship services of the church. Adequate leadership should be provided to make the choirs worth-while.

A church in which many experiences in music are offered, and in which people participate wholeheartedly, is a vital, warm, friendly church.

Music is truly the "handmaid of religion." It is to be enjoyed in meaningful participation.

> "Sing praises to God, sing praises!
> Sing praises to our King, sing praises!
> For God is the king of all the earth;
> sing praises with a psalm!"
>
> *Ps. 47:6, 7.*

BIBLIOGRAPHY

BIBLIOGRAPHY

Music in the Church

Church Music in History and Practice, by Winfred Douglas. Charles Scribner's Sons, 1937.

Music in Worship, by Walter S. Swisher. Oliver Ditson Co.

The Arts and Religion, edited by Albert E. Bailey. The Macmillan Company, 1944. Chapter III, "The Expression of Religion in Music," by H. Augustine Smith.

Our Singing Church, by Hubert V. Taylor and John Milton Kelly. Board of Christian Education, Presbyterian Church in the U.S.A., 1951.

Music and Worship, A Manual for the Organist and the Choir Director, by Federal Lee Whittlesey. Board of Christian Education, Presbyterian Church in the U.S.A., 1949.

The Problems of Music in the Church, by Waldo Selden Pratt. Bulletin IV, Department of Church and Choral Music, Northwestern University.

"The Sacrament of Music," by Robert B. Lee, in *Union Seminary Quarterly Review,* Vol. IV, No. 2, January, 1949.

Worship — the Bible

The Bible. Revised Standard Version, 1952.

Worship, by Evelyn Underhill. Harper & Brothers.

The Literature of the Old Testament, by Julius A. Bewer. Columbia University Records of Civilization, Columbia University Press, 1933.

Guideposts to Creative Family Worship, by Edward W. and Anna Laura Gebhard. Abingdon Press, 1953.

Hymns and Poetry

Lyric Religion, by H. Augustine Smith. Fleming H. Revell Company, 1931.

The Gospel in Hymns, by Albert E. Bailey. Charles Scribner's Sons, 1950.

The Minister and the Hymnal, Bulletin VI. Department of Church and Choral Music, Northwestern University, 1933.

The Hymnal. Presbyterian Board of Christian Education, 1933.

Handbook to The Hymnal (Presbyterian), edited by William C. Covert and Calvin W. Laufer. Presbyterian Board of Christian Education, 1935.

Our Hymnody, A Manual of the Methodist Hymnal, by Robert G. McCutchan. The Methodist Book Concern, 1937.

The Methodist Hymnal. The Methodist Book Concern, 1935.

One Hundred and One Hymn Stories, by Carl F. Price. Abingdon Press, 1923.

The Hymn Festival Movement in America, by Reginald McAll. The Hymn Society of America, 1951.

Beyond the Tonal Horizon of Music, by Frederick William Schlieder. Printed in San Francisco by Wallace Kibbe & Sons; distributed by Seminary Book Shop, 3041 Broadway, New York 27, New York, 1948.

Music and Christian Education

The Teaching Ministry of the Church, by James D. Smart. The Westminster Press, 1954.

Music in Christian Education, A Manual for Leaders in Church and Church School, by Edith Lovell Thomas. Abingdon Press, 1953.

Music in the Religious Growth of Children, by Elizabeth McE. Shields. Abingdon Press, 1943.

Guiding Boys and Girls to Christ, by Ralph Mould. Board of Christian Education, Presbyterian Church in the U.S.A., 1953.

Christian Education in Our Church, A Manual for the Organization and Administration of a Unified Program of Christian Education in the Individual Church. Board of Christian Education, Presbyterian Church in the U.S.A.

A series of books on Christian education at the age levels of children, published by the Board of Christian Education of the Presbyterian Church, U.S.A.

When They Are Three, by Sara G. Klein, 1950.

When They Are Four and Five, by Kathrene McLandress Tobey, 1950.

When They Are Six to Eight, by Eva Watson Frye, 1950.

When They Are Nine to Eleven, by Florence Martin, 1950.

The Children We Teach, by Elizabeth S. Whitehouse. Judson Press, 1950.

A Study of Young Children, by Ruth Strang. Abingdon Press, 1944.

Nursery Children in the Church, by Gertrude Andon. Prepared for the Department of Children's Work, Division of Christian Education of the Congregational-Christian Churches. Pilgrim Press, 1945.

Religious Nurture in Nursery Class and Home, by Mary Edna Lloyd. Whitmore and Stone, 1942.

Ways Youth Learn, Clarice Bowman. Harper & Brothers, 1952.

Discipline

Discipline for Freedom, Service Bulletin No. 23. Association for Childhood Education International, 1200 Fifteenth Street N.W., Washington 5, D.C., 1950–1951.

Discipline Through Affection, by Aline B. Auerbach. Child Study Association of America, Inc., 132 E. 74th St., New York 21, N.Y., 1951.

New Ways in Discipline, by Dorothy Baruch. Whittlesey House, McGraw-Hill Book Company, Inc., 1949.

Why Children Misbehave, by Charles W. Leonard. Science Research Associates, Inc., 1953.

These Are Your Children (expanded edition), by Jenkins, Shacter, and Bauer. Scott, Foresman and Company.

Living with Teeners, by Grace Sloan Overton. Broadman Press, 1950.

Teenagers — Their Days and Ways. National Council of Churches of Christ in the U.S.A., 1952.

The Diapason magazine, March, 1955. S. E. Gruenstein, Editor-Publisher, 1511 Kimball Building, Wabash Avenue and Jackson Blvd., Chicago 4, Ill.

Music and Children

Children and Music, by Beatrice Landeck. William Sloane Associates, Inc., 1952.

Children and Music, Bulletin of the Association for Childhood Education International, 1200 Fifteenth Street N.W., Washington 5, D.C., 1948.

Living Music with Children, by Mary Barrett. National Association for Nursery Education, 1951.

Rhythmic Experiences

Rhythms and Dances, by Sister Ann Harvey. G. Schirmer, Inc., 1944.

How to Teach the Rhythm Band, by Angela Diller and Kate S. Page. G. Schirmer, Inc.

Music Participation in the Secondary School, by Beatrice P. and Max T. Krone. Neil A. Kjos Music Co., 1952.

The Music Hour in Kindergarten and First Grade. Silver, Burdett & Company, 1929.

Kindergarten Book, by Dorothy Bell Briggs. Oliver Ditson Co., 1941.

Rhythmic Sketches, by Ruth Cawthorne Vesper. The Willis Music Co., 1929.

Creative Rhythmic Movement for Children, by Gladys Andrews. Prentice-Hall, Inc., 1954.

Creative Music

First Steps in Playing and Composing, A Music Book for Children, by Satis N. Coleman. John Day Co., Inc., 1930.

Creative Music for Children, by Satis N. Coleman. G. P. Putnam's Sons.

Creative Music in the Home, by Satis N. Coleman. Lewis E. Meyers and Co., 1928.

The Book of Bells, by Satis N. Coleman. John Day Co., Inc., 1938.

Creative School Music, by Lillian M. Fox and Levi T. Hopkins. Silver, Burdett & Company, 1936.

Listening Experiences

The American Record Guide. 115 Reed Avenue, Pelham 65, N.Y.

Children and Records, Pamphlet by National Council of Churches of

Christ in the U.S.A. Division of Christian Education, 79 E. Adams St., Chicago 3, Ill.

Children and Music, Bulletin of Association for Childhood Education International, 1200 Fifteenth St. N.W., Washington 5, D.C., 1948.

There's Music in Children, by Emma Sheehy. Henry Holt & Co., Inc., 1946.

Listening to Music, by Douglas S. Moore. W. W. Norton & Company, Inc., 1937.

Audio-Visual Resource Guide. National Council of Churches of Christ in the U.S.A., 79 E. Adams St., Chicago, Ill., 1955.

Musical Moments in Worship, edited by Edith Lovell Thomas. Abingdon Press, 1936.

The Victor Record Catalogue, Educational Records.

The Columbia Record Catalogue.

Selected References:

"Rhythmic Activity with Records," by Mary Robison, in *Opening Doors,* April–June, 1953.

"Listening," by Edna Stover, in *Opening Doors,* April–June, 1950.

"Listening," by Edna Stover, in *Opening Doors,* January–March, 1950.

"Records for Your Children and You," by Emma Sheehy, in *Parent's Magazine,* Nov., 1947.

How to Listen to Music, by H. E. Krehbiel. Charles Scribner's Sons, 1922.

From Song to Symphony, by Daniel Gregory Mason. Oliver Ditson Co., 1924.

Sources of Songs

The Little Singing Time, by Satis N. Coleman and Alice G. Thorn. John Day Co., Inc., 1940.

Singing Time, by Satis N. Coleman and Alice G. Thorn. John Day Co., Inc., 1929.

Another Singing Time, by Satis N. Coleman and Alice G. Thorn. John Day Co., Inc., 1937.

Songs for the Nursery School, by L. P. McCarteney. The Willis Music Co., 1937.

Sing, Children, Sing (primary), by Edith Lovell Thomas. Abingdon Press, 1939.

Martin and Judy Songs (preschool), by Edith Lovell Thomas. Beacon Press.

The Whole World Singing, by Edith Lovell Thomas. Friendship Press, 1950.

Songs Children Like. Association for Childhood Education International, 1200 Fifteenth St., N.W., Washington, D.C., 1954.

Fun and Folk Songs (revised). The Westminster Press, 1949.

Fun and Festival Series, Friendship Press.

Music of One World (United Nations Songs for U.S. Singing), published by Cooperative Recreational Service.

American Folk Songs for Children, by Ruth Crawford Seeger. Doubleday & Co., Inc., 1948.

Finger Plays, by Emilie Poulsson. Lothrop, Lee & Shepard Co., Inc.

The Complete Nursery Song Book, by Inez Bertail. Lothrop, Lee & Shepard Co., Inc., 1947.

GRADED HYMNALS

By The Westminster Press:
- *When the Little Child Wants to Sing,* 1935.
- *Hymns for Primary Worship,* 1946.
- *Hymns for Junior Worship,* 1940.
- *The Hymnal for Youth,* 1941.

Singing Worship with Boys and Girls (junior), edited by Edith Lovell Thomas. Abingdon Press, 1935.

The New Hymnal for American Youth, edited by H. Augustine Smith. Fleming H. Revell Company, 1953.

VOICE

Read This and Sing! for Voice Students, Chorus and Choir Singers, by Clyde R. Dengler. Teacher's manual; student's manual. Theodore Presser Co., 1945.

Vocal Artistry, by Peter Tkach. Teacher's manual; student's manual. Neil A. Kjos Music Co. A guide to the development of artistic solo and ensemble singing.

Thirty-six Lessons in Singing, by Herbert Witherspoon. Chicago Miessner Institute, 1930.

The Renaissance of the Vocal Art, by Edmund J. Meyer. G. Schirmer, Inc., 1902.

Clear-cut Speech in Song, by Clara Kathleen Rogers. Oliver Ditson Co.

Choirs

"The Ministry of Music" — Series I, Youth Choirs, by Federal Lee Whittlesey. Series II, Senior Choirs, by Federal Lee Whittlesey. Board of Christian Education, Presbyterian Church in the U.S.A.

The Successful Children's Choir, by Ruth Krehbiel Jacobs. H. T. FitzSimons Co., revised, 1948.

Steps Toward a Singing Church, by Donald Kettring. The Westminster Press, 1948.

Music Theory and Interpretation

First Year Musical Theory, by Thomas Tapper. The Arthur P Schmidt Co., 1912.

Harmony, by Walter Piston. W. W. Norton & Company, Inc., 1941.

The Language of Music, by Klaus Liepmann. The Ronald Press Co., 1953.

Listening to Music Creatively, by E. J. Stringham, Prentice-Hall, Inc.

The School Music Conductor, by Paul Van Bodegraven and Harry Robert Wilson. Hall & McCreary Company.

Choral Conducting, by Archibald T. Davison, Harvard University Press, 1940.

The Chorus and Its Conductor, by Max T. Krone. Neil A. Kjos Music Co., 1945.

Interpretation in Song, by H. Plunket Greene. The Macmillan Company, 1921.

Choral Speech

The Speech Choir, by Marjorie Gullan. Harper & Brothers, 1937.

Playmaking with Children, by Winifred Ward. Appleton-Century-Crofts, Inc., 1947.

Choral Readings for Worship and Inspiration, edited by Helen A. Brown and Harry J. Heltman. The Westminster Press, 1954.

Choral Readings from the Bible, edited by Helen A. Brown and Harry J. Heltman. The Westminster Press, 1955.

Choral Readings for Fun and Recreation, edited by Helen A. Brown and Harry J. Heltman. The Westminster Press, 1956.